LEVERAGE
COMPETENCIES

The Key to Financial Leadership Success

Frederick C. Militello, Jr.

Michael D. Schwalberg

A publication of Financial Executives Research Foundation, Inc.

Financial Executives Research Foundation, Inc.
10 Madison Avenue
P.O. Box 1938
Morristown, New Jersey 07962-1938
(973) 898-4608

International Standard Book Number 1-885065-20-5
Library of Congress Control Number 00-136078
Printed in the United States of America

First Printing

Financial Executives Research Foundation, Inc. is the research affiliate of Financial Executives International. The purpose of the Foundation is to sponsor research and publish informative material in the field of business management, with particular emphasis on the practice of financial management and its evolving role in the management of business.

Research Foundation publications can be ordered by calling 1-800-680-FERF (U.S. and Canada only; international orders, please call 770-751-1986). Quantity discounts are available.

ADVISORY COMMITTEE

Lawrence J. Piano (Chairman)
Vice President
Lincoln National Intermediaries, Inc.
Lincoln Re Financial Strategies Group

Gracie F. Hemphill
Director—Research
Financial Executives Research Foundation, Inc.

Douglas R. Maughan
Finance
W. L. Gore & Associates, Inc.

Katherine L. Parker
Director, Business Effectiveness
Nortel Networks Corporation

Cynthia Waller Vallario
Project Manager
Financial Executives Research Foundation, Inc.

Rhona L. Ferling
Publications Manager
Financial Executives Research Foundation, Inc.

C O N T E N T S

Introduction

Research Background

The mandate to transform finance into a force for organizational change and business effectiveness has clearly been issued. In response, the Financial Executives Research Foundation has conducted research that has changed the direction of financial practices. Beginning with *Changing Roles of Financial Management: Getting Close to the Business* (1990), and subsequently with *The Empowered Organization: Redefining the Roles and Practices of Finance* (1994), these studies have helped financial executives climb out of their silos and begin integrating themselves into the business lives of their organizations.

Although the leadership challenge for financial executives is now clear, uncertainty remains: Do financial executives really have the full range of **competencies**[1] to make this leadership mandate a reality? Moreover, in our eagerness to embrace changing roles and a new mandate for finance—without fully addressing such competencies—are we actually setting the stage for future disappointments and failures? These concerns, expressed by corporate CEOs and CFOs alike, are increasingly rising to the surface.

One of the most noteworthy surveys of financial practices offers the following observation, critical to the future leadership success of all finance executives:[2]

> We categorize the competencies CFOs require as foundation and leverage. **Foundation competencies** are professional, technical and control related—these are the minimum competencies for all CFOs. In contrast, **leverage competencies**[3] allow CFOs to build both the business (strategic thinking, innovation, managing business risk and change) and personal relationships (teamwork and **coaching,** inspiring leadership). Our research shows that most, if

not all, CFOs rate themselves competent in foundation attributes. But many see further scope for personal development in leverage competencies.... Of all business functions, finance tends to lead fastest to the boardroom. This leaves precious little time for planned personal development. *The CFO's leverage competencies tend to be acquired haphazardly or neglected altogether.* (Emphasis added.)

The importance of competencies, and the new challenge of leadership outlined above, is echoed by the following quote regarding the requirements of leadership in the twenty-first century:[4]

The truly successful managers and leaders of the next century will be determined not by what they know but by how fast they can learn.... They will excel not by possessing traditional skills and tools but by demonstrating a high degree of flexibility and adaptability in dealing with both technology and people and by being able to stay constantly meaningfully connected to others in the ever-changing world.

The difference between 1990 and 2000 will probably be less extreme than the differences between 2000 and 2010, as we experience a world that that is demanding not only of a rethinking of management competencies, but a fundamental redefinition of the social contract between employer and employee, between colleague and colleague, between worker and work itself.

Research Objectives

Leadership development is a challenge for all professionals. However, for finance executives, no book has been written, nor research undertaken, specifically addressing their behavioral or leadership development. This research seeks to correct these omissions by:

- Articulating clearly the critical skills and competencies finance executives need to become effective partners and business leaders of their organizations.

- Illustrating the ways in which these competencies are being developed, achieved, and maintained by "work-in-progress"[5] companies.

- Indicating the greatest challenges in achieving these competencies and how these skills are—or are not—being successfully practiced.

- Noting which competencies seem to be critical for different levels of financial executive responsibility and how these competencies change as one advances in the organization.

- Suggesting the most effective ways for finance executives, whether they are from large or middle-market organizations, to achieve these skills.

- Offering ideas for what works and what does not in crafting a new paradigm of leadership behavior and performance expectations for finance executives of the future.

Research Participants

In selecting the company participants, we examined three groups of potential candidates. Each brings a unique perspective to the developmental challenges of our research. The criteria used to select the work-in-progress case-study companies are as follows:

The first group of candidates included organizations that participated in the Foundation's 1994 research, *The Empowered Organization: Redefining the Roles and Practices of the Financial Executive.*[6] These companies were CoreStates Financial Corporation, Corning, W. L. Gore & Associates, Harley-Davidson, Geo. E. Keith Company, Herman Miller, Levi Strauss & Company, and Silicon Graphics. Each of these organizations was committed early on to the advancement of today's finance executive as a true business partner and facilitator of shareholder value.

From this first group of research candidates, we selected W. L. Gore & Associates to participate in the current research. Besides bringing a "past-study" perspective to the research, Gore's participation is noteworthy because it has been consistently selected as one of the best companies to work for in America.[7]

The second group of candidates included those organizations whose commitment to leadership development has been well documented,[8] but whose approach to the development of finance leaders has had little or no mention. These companies include Asea Brown Boveri, Canon, General Electric, IBM, Intel, Kao Corporation, Solvay Polymers, Unilever, and a wide range of other global organizations.

From this second group, we selected Solvay Polymers and Unilever. This research explores how these leading-edge companies have incorporated the importance of a wide range of competencies into the developmental paths and career expectations of their finance executives.

The third group of candidates included organizations that have received noteworthy attention for making the leadership development of their finance executives a key organizational priority,[9] but that have not communicated the details of how they facilitate this development. These companies include Air Products and Chemicals, Bristol-Myers Squibb Company, Chrysler, Dana Corporation, Caterpillar, General Public Utilities, Lucent Technologies, Nortel Networks, Procter & Gamble, Southern New England Telecommunications, Synovus Financial Corp., and Whirlpool.

From this third group, we selected Air Products and Chemicals, Bristol-Myers Squibb, Dana Corporation, Nortel Networks, and Synovus Financial Corp.

In-depth interviews were conducted at the corporate headquarters of each of the eight participants. These interviews were based on a detailed research questionnaire protocol.[10] More than 30 in-depth interviews were conducted with high-level finance, human resources, and business line professionals.

Summary

The research you are about to read is not a study of finance written by finance professionals for finance professionals. Rather, it is a study that seeks to uncover the collaborative efforts that companies are implementing—or struggling with—to help finance executives understand the new realities of leadership and the behavioral changes required of them. It is about effective leadership behavior and what it will take to ensure that finance executives can meet the lofty business challenges and shareholder initiatives with which they are increasingly confronted. Because of its content and implications, this study will no doubt affect both the professional and personal lives of those choosing to consider and pursue its findings.

Endnotes

1. Terms in **bold** type are defined in the glossary.

2. Price Waterhouse Financial and Cost Management Team, *CFO: Architect of the Corporation's Future* (New York: John Wiley & Sons, 1997), 278–279. This report is based on the Conference Board/Price Waterhouse survey *CFO 2000: The Global CFO as Strategic Business Partner.* See the annotated bibliography for further details on this reference.

3. We use the phrase "leverage competencies" to refer to those behaviors that tend to increase the influence and leadership role of finance executives throughout the business lives of their organizations. See chapter 2 for a discussion of these competencies.

4. Mark Nevins and S. Stumpf, "21st-Century Leadership: Redefining Management Education," *Business Strategy,* no. 16 (third quarter 1999): 42–43.

5. The participating case study organizations are called "work-in-progress" companies rather than the too-common nomenclature "best practice." Companies in this study seemed more comfortable with this classification. None considered their work in the field of leadership development to be complete or entirely learned. Moreover, all expressed that their efforts were ongoing and special to the culture and values of their organizations. Most important, each remained open to discussing its shortcomings, was eager to learn more, and was willing to share its experiences and lessons learned with others.

6. H. A. Davis and F. C. Militello, *The Empowered Organization: Redefining the Roles and Practices of Finance* (Morristown, NJ: Financial Executives Research Foundation, 1994). See the annotated bibliography for further details on this reference.

7. See "The 100 Best Companies to Work for in America," *Fortune.* The magazine has published the survey annually since 1998.

8. A good example of this documentation is the scholarly work by S. Ghoshal and C. Bartlett, *The Individualized Corporation: A Fundamentally New Approach to Management* (HarperCollins: New York, 1997).

9. For example see, S. Barr, "Sometimes a Great Notion," *CFO* (May 1998): 40–50, as well as the *Fortune* survey noted above.

10. This protocol is included as an appendix and can be used as a finance executive leadership "audit" or checklist for existing company practices.

Emotional Competencies:
The *Sine Qua Non* of Leadership

I n 1973, David McClelland, a psychologist at Harvard University, published "Testing for Competence Rather than Intelligence."[1] In this paper, he argued that traditional markers of intelligence quotient (IQ)—academic aptitude, knowledge, and achievement—were poor predictors of job performance and success in general. McClelland maintained that sets of competencies were much more useful in predicting success on the job. This paper launched a new approach to the study of "excellence."[2] It is an approach that examines and measures qualities, attributes, and behaviors that lead to superior job performance.

A competency may be defined as a personal trait or set of habits that are causally related to effective or superior job performance.[3] These underlying characteristics are stable, enduring patterns or styles of behavior, thought, and emotions. Lyle Spencer, a student of McClelland, and his colleagues[4] have continued work on delineating and measuring competencies that distinguish superior job performance across a variety of jobs and professions.

Spencer and Spencer assert that the type or level of a competency has important implications for human resource planning. Knowledge and skill competencies (e.g., computer programming) are surface characteristics; motive (e.g., achievement orientation), trait (e.g., emotional self-control), and self-concept (e.g., self-confidence) competencies run deeper, or are more core to one's personality. According to these researchers, knowledge and skill competencies can be readily developed. Self-concept competencies can be developed but take more time and energy. Motives and traits are the most core to one's personality, and it may be more cost-effective for an organization to select for these competencies rather than attempt to develop them.

The majority of competencies found to be predictive of superior job performance have been intrapersonal (e.g., self-control, adaptability) and interpersonal (e.g., relationship building, persuasiveness) in nature, as opposed to **cognitive competencies** (e.g., analytical thinking, conceptual thinking). This finding led another of McClelland's former students, Daniel Goleman, to focus on **emotional intelligence,** composed of **emotional competencies.**

Emotional Intelligence

Since the publication of Goleman's book, *Emotional Intelligence: Why It Can Matter More than IQ,*[5] the term emotional intelligence, or emotional intelligence quotient (EQ) has become part of our vocabulary. Goleman notes that his work builds on that of others. Peter Salovey and John Mayer were among the first to coin the term.[6] They defined it "in terms of being able to monitor and regulate one's own and others' feelings, and to use feelings to guide thoughts and action."[7] In his book *Working with Emotional Intelligence,* Goleman adapted the concept to work life, incorporating the work on competencies that he, McClelland, and McClelland's colleagues and former students had done.

Goleman describes emotional intelligence as follows:

> [T]he capacity for recognizing our feelings and those of others, for motivating ourselves, and for managing emotions well in ourselves and in our relationships. It describes abilities distinct from, but complementary to, academic intelligence, the purely cognitive capacities measured by IQ. Many people who are book smart but lack emotional intelligence end up working for people who have lower IQs than they but who excel in emotional intelligence skills.[8]

Goleman does not dismiss IQ as unimportant. Rather, he views IQ and technical expertise as **threshold competencies.** A certain level of IQ and knowledge or technical expertise is necessary to get you in the door. But once you're in the door, it is EQ and EQ competencies that separate the star performers from the average ones. Goleman and others have backed up this assertion with data gathered from hundreds of companies. Research methods that McClelland and his colleagues developed[9] include differentiating outstanding performers from average ones, extensively interviewing and testing outstanding performers, and comparing their performance on a variety of capabilities. The result is a list of competencies that predicts success on the job.

Overall, emotional competencies were found to be twice as important for job success as cognitive competencies. Furthermore, emotional competencies become more important the higher one goes in the organization. Among the competencies found to distinguish star leaders were *influence, team leadership, political awareness, self-confidence,* and *drive for achievement.*

In addition, while certain cognitive competencies such as *strategic vision* may be important, emotional competencies are required to use them to their full potential. For example, Ronald Heifitz of Harvard University, an authority on leadership, notes, "With leaders, the sense of sight—vision—is closely linked to the sense of hearing."[10] That is, effective listening skills, among other emotional competencies, are central to the implementation of one's vision. Similarly, in discussing visionary CFOs, J. Rucker McCarty, partner-in-charge of the CFO practice at Heidrick & Struggles, states, "While generating and shaping a vision is difficult, imparting it may be even trickier.... The person who does so has to be charismatic and have communication skills to sell that vision to the CEO and others in the company."[11]

Emotional Competencies

An emotional competency is "a learned capability based on emotional intelligence that results in outstanding performance at work."[12] While labeled emotional competencies, they encompass thoughts, feelings, and behaviors.

Goleman breaks down emotional intelligence into five elements or dimensions: self-awareness, self-regulation, motivation, empathy, and social skills. The 25 emotional competencies Goleman outlines are clustered into groups based on the element underlying each competency. In addition, the emotional competencies are divided into two categories: personal competencies, which relate to how we manage ourselves, and social competencies, which determine our skill in relating to others. Table 2.1 outlines Goleman's "emotional competence

Table 2.1
The Emotional Competence Framework

PERSONAL COMPETENCE

These competencies determine how we manage ourselves.

Self-Awareness
Knowing one's internal states, preferences, resources, and intuitions

- *Emotional awareness:* Recognizing one's emotions and their effects
- *Accurate self-assessment:* Knowing one's strengths and limits
- *Self-confidence:* A strong sense of one's self-worth and capabilities

Self-Regulation
Managing one's internal states, impulses, and resources

- *Self-control:* Keeping disruptive emotions and impulses in check
- *Trustworthiness:* Maintaining standards of honesty and integrity
- *Conscientiousness:* Taking responsibility for personal performance
- *Adaptability:* Flexibility in handling change
- *Innovation:* Being comfortable with novel ideas, approaches, and new information

Motivation
Emotional tendencies that guide or facilitate reaching goals

- *Achievement drive:* Striving to improve or meet a standard of excellence
- *Commitment:* Aligning with the goals of the group or organization
- *Initiative:* Readiness to act on opportunities
- *Optimism:* Persistence in pursuing goals despite obstacles and setbacks

SOCIAL COMPETENCE

These competencies determine how we handle relationships

Empathy
Awareness of others' feelings, needs, and concerns

- *Understanding others:* Sensing others' feelings and perspectives, and taking an active interest in their concerns
- *Developing others:* Sensing others' development needs and bolstering their abilities
- *Service orientation:* Anticipating, recognizing, and meeting customers' needs
- *Leveraging diversity:* Cultivating opportunities through different kinds of people
- *Political awareness:* Reading a group's emotional currents and power relationships

Table 2.1
The Emotional Competence Framework (Continued)

Social Skills
Adeptness at inducing desirable responses in others

- *Influence:* Wielding effective tactics for persuasion
- *Communication:* Listening openly and sending convincing messages
- *Conflict management:* Negotiating and resolving disagreements
- *Leadership:* Inspiring and guiding individuals and groups
- *Change catalyst:* Initiating or managing change
- *Building bonds:* Nurturing instrumental relationships
- *Collaboration and cooperation:* Working with others toward shared goals
- *Team capabilities:* Creating group synergy in pursuing collective goals

Source: D. Goleman. *Working with Emotional Intelligence*, pp. 26–27. Reprinted with permission from Bantam Books.

framework,"[13] defining each of the five elements and their related emotional competencies.

This is a generic list of competencies. Each of us has a competency profile of strengths and limitations. Superior job performance requires strengths in a number of competencies across the five elements of emotional intelligence. Different jobs at different organizations will, of course, require diverse sets of competencies at various levels of mastery. **Competency models,** which arrive at those sets of competencies most predictive of superior job performance for a given group, can be developed for an individual company.

The following sections discuss each of the five elements of emotional intelligence on which the competencies are based.[14]

Self-Awareness

Self-awareness is an important foundation on which many, if not most, emotional competencies are supported. Individuals who are *emotionally self-aware* possess a firm grasp of their emotions, drives, and needs. They understand how these affect their thoughts, behaviors, and job performance. They also understand the effect of their feelings and beliefs on others. Such people are aware of their guiding values and goals and tend to behave in a manner that is consistent with their values.

People strong in *accurate self-assessment* know their strengths and limitations. They tend to leverage their strengths and compensate for limitations. They are not afraid to share these limitations and know when to work with others who are strong in capabilities they may lack.

Another hallmark of those strong in self-awareness is *self-confidence.* People who are self-confident project self-assurance and have presence. They are decisive and willing to express unpopular opinions, especially those that are consistent with their personal values.

Self-Regulation

People strong in self-regulation *control their feelings and impulses* rather than letting themselves be controlled by them. Such individuals are unflappable in the face of frustration, disappointment, or stress. In fact, they may thrive under stress, channeling it into productivity.

Leaders strong in this element of emotional intelligence facilitate an environment of trust. They do so in part because such in-control types tend to be more trustworthy themselves. They are reliable, well-organized, conscientious, and unlikely to be loose cannons. They are more likely to maintain high standards of honesty and integrity than their more impulsive counterparts.

People high in self-regulation tend to be more *adaptable* and *innovative.* They do not panic in the face of change. Thoughtful and reflective, they listen, gather information, and can then behave in a strategic manner.

Motivation

Motivated individuals are results-oriented and set challenging goals for themselves and their organizations. They constantly strive to enhance their performance and keep careful track of their success or lack thereof. They are forever seeking ways to improve their performance; feedback and data gathering are a means to that end. Self-assessment/self-awareness is an integral part of the data they gather.

Those high in motivation tend to be committed to the organization. Says Goleman, "When people love their job for the work itself, they often feel committed to the organizations that make that work possible."[15] Those who are highly committed to an organization make the organization's goals their goals. They thrive best in an organization with a clear, authentic, well-formulated mission and core values.

Finally, people high in motivation tend to be persistent, proactive, and *optimistic.* These people focus on approaching success, not avoiding failure. They see failures as setbacks that are attributable, not to an unchangeable personal flaw, but to temporary circumstances or factors over which they ultimately have some control.

Empathy

Empathy involves the awareness and understanding of others' feelings, needs, perspectives, and concerns. The term has an emotional connotation that belies its importance to business. Without empathy, leaders will be out of touch with their subordinates, peers, supervisors, and customers.

Goleman maintains that empathy has become especially important for today's leaders for a number of reasons. For example, cross-functional teams have increasingly come into use in corporations. Team members come from a variety of backgrounds, with different personalities, styles, hidden agendas, and baggage. Sensing and understanding the needs and perspectives of everyone on the team helps the leader navigate through potentially rough waters, especially when the teams are charged with reaching a consensus.

Globalization and diversity issues also require a high level of empathy. Without a deep appreciation and understanding of cross-cultural and diversity issues, misunderstandings, alienation, and ultimately loss of productivity and business can result. Empathic leaders can *leverage diversity.* They see diversity as an opportunity rather than a hindrance and foster an environment in which diverse people can thrive.

In a similar vein, empathy is fundamental to reading and understanding political and social currents affecting an organization. Leaders strong in this skill detect where the real power and influence lie. They pick up on crucial social networks. They understand the internal and external forces that influence not just their organization, but their customers and competition as well. Leaders who are *politically astute* are attuned to an organization's culture and climate and its informal power structure.

Empathy can play a role in developing and retaining a company's most important resource—its people. As noted, empathy is central to rapport. Leaders who are not just supervisors, but are also seen as **mentors** or coaches, foster increased commitment and job satisfaction. They stretch people, challenging them with growth opportunities and expecting the best from them.

Finally, empathy is at the core of a strong *service orientation*. People who demonstrate this competency have a keen understanding of a customer's needs. They actively seek to satisfy those needs and gain customer satisfaction and loyalty. Just as empathy allows leaders to develop rapport with those they coach, people strong in service orientation tend to develop rapport with customers, both internal and external. Gaining rapport and trust with one's customers is, of course, invaluable to a company.

Social Skill

Social skill, as stated in table 2.1, involves "adeptness at inducing desirable responses in others." Of all the components of emotional intelligence, this is the most self-evident in terms of being critical to effective leadership. Social skill is built on the other components. But without social skill, most of the other components become meaningless in terms of effective leadership.

Influence is at the core of leadership. People with this competency are skilled at persuasion and rapport building. Such leaders are adept at building consensus rather than simply imposing their will or ideas on others. They are often skilled at shaping and presenting information so that those around them come to the desired conclusions on their own. It should be noted that the leader who influences solely for personal gain will usually not be as effective as one who does so for the sake of others. Commitment is more likely to come when people perceive a leader as caring about them, the organization, or a higher cause.

The leader who wishes to influence must know how to communicate. *Communication* is not as simple a competency to master as some may think. Says Goleman, "The single biggest complaint of American workers is poor communication with management; two-thirds say it prevents them from doing their best work."[16]

An effective communicator sends out clear, cogent, convincing messages. Much of effective communicating, however, is about listening. Good listeners are active listeners. They communicate that they hear what people are saying and respect their opinions, even if they may not agree. They may do so by asking astute questions of the speaker or giving feedback that communicates an accurate understanding of the points being made, and possibly, even of the emotions and issues behind the points. Leaders skilled in communication will foster an atmosphere of openness and acceptance of diverse ideas. They welcome or seek out feedback or ideas and reward communication and the open sharing of information.

Conflict management is another core social skill competency. People with this competency are not only adept at handling conflict, they tend to be able to anticipate it, bring potential conflict or disagreement out into the open, and de-escalate it. They work toward win-win solutions if possible. Of course, a variety of capabilities, such as self-confidence, empathy, communication, and influence, will come into play here.

Leadership itself is a social skill competency. According to Goleman, those strong in this competency are able to articulate a vision or mission and arouse enthusiasm for it. They can lead even in the absence of formal power. While inspiring and guiding others, they also expect the best of them and hold them accountable. Good leaders lead by example. They are a source of the organization's positive energy or emotional tone. They are flexible in their approach to leadership—tough when necessary, warm and empathic when appropriate.

Effective leaders are not just comfortable with change, they can be *change catalysts.* Such people need not have been the originators of the idea for change, but they recognize the need for it and are not afraid to challenge the status quo. They champion change and mobilize key stakeholders in its pursuit.

Building bonds, collaboration and cooperation, and *team capabilities* are especially important for effectively collaborating with others and working on teams. People strong in building bonds cultivate and nurture informal social/professional networks. They have a talent for connecting with others and make an effort to do so. They use these connections to their fullest. The collaboration and cooperation competency is marked by the desire and ability to pool information and resources with others. Such people tend to foster an amicable, cooperative climate. Finally, people high in team capabilities have a talent for maximizing team effectiveness. They model qualities such as cooperation, mutual respect, effective listening skills, and credit sharing, which tend to make a team more successful. Regarding competent team leaders, says Goleman,

> The best leaders are able to get everyone to buy into a common sense of mission, goals, and agenda. The ability to articulate a compelling vision that serves as the guiding force for the group may be the single most important contribution of a good team leader. A charismatic team leader can hold a team on course when all else fails.[17]

The Emotionally Intelligent Organization

An analysis of exceptional companies identified eight common practices among them:[18]

- A balance between the human and financial sides of the company's agenda
- Organizational commitment to a basic strategy
- Initiative to stimulate improvements in performance
- Open communication and trust building with all stakeholders
- Building relationships inside and outside that offer competitive advantage
- Collaboration, support, and sharing resources
- Innovation, risk taking, and learning together
- A passion for competition and continual improvement

The organizational competencies common to top-performing companies bear a striking resemblance to those found among top-performing individuals.

Emotional competencies displayed by emotionally intelligent individuals may also apply to the **emotionally intelligent organization,** says Goleman. Recall the discussion of communication and the ubiquitous complaint by workers of the lack of communication within organizations. An emotionally intelligent organization promotes communication at all levels.

A self-aware organization knows its values and vision. Its mission statement is not just lip service. It knows its strengths and weaknesses and whether or not it is living up to its values. An empathic organization has a feel for the needs and perspectives of its people. A company can create an atmosphere of fear and cynicism or a sense of shared mission and drive to achieve. It can be rigid or flexible, discourage diversity or leverage it.

Of course, there is an interaction between the level of emotional competencies an organization displays and those its members, especially its leaders, display. An emotionally competent leader will create a positive, productive work environment. An emotionally intelligent work environment will attract and retain emotionally competent people.

Developing Emotional Competencies

As discussed earlier, Spencer and Spencer maintain that some competencies may be more easily developed than others. That is, some competencies, such as communication and conflict management, involve teachable skills. Others, such as achievement drive and self-confidence, are more core to one's personality; it may be more cost-effective to select for these deeper competencies rather than attempt to develop them.

Goleman asserts that all emotional competencies can, to some extent, be developed. He described, for example, how Lyle Spencer and his colleagues trained assembly-line workers at an automobile company to raise their need to achieve. Apparently, this training was so successful that most of the workers ended up quitting their jobs and starting their own businesses.

Emotional intelligence is a product of both nature and nurture. Research indicates that there is a genetic component to emotional intelligence. As with IQ, some of us may be born with a higher or lower EQ than others. On the other hand, environment also plays a strong role in its development. Emotional intelligence actually increases with age. "There is an old-fashioned word for the phenomenon: maturity."[19]

Thus, while IQ remains relatively fixed throughout life, EQ continues to develop over time and can be taught at any age.

Studies of the brain indicate that EQ emanates from different areas of the brain than IQ. Knowledge of these areas sheds important light on emotional competency development. Simply put, experience, not book learning, is most important for the development of emotional competencies. Training for these competencies will not be effective if it involves only the storage of new information. For an executive who wishes to overcome a fear of public speaking, it is not enough simply to read pointers on giving effective public presentations. She or he must actually give public presentations, again and again.

An in-depth exposition of the science (and art) of behavior change, which also involves change in thoughts and feelings, is beyond the scope of this chapter. Goleman and his colleagues, however, have established best practice guidelines for teaching emotional competencies.[20]

The first step in emotional competency training is a thorough assessment. This should include *assessing the job* to determine which competencies are important for superior job performance. Training can focus on those competencies and any other capabilities that support them.

Assessing the individual involves determining a profile of competency strengths and limitations. Multiple assessment tools may be employed here. A useful process, used more and more frequently, is a **360-degree feedback evaluation,** which involves gathering information from an individual's supervisor(s), peers, and subordinates. An **assessment center** includes, among other things, direct observation of an individual or group of individuals in job simulations. Individually, each tool or method is fallible. For example, 360-degree feedback can be affected by office politics. Multiple assessment methods should be used, allowing for information to converge from a variety of sources.

One must *gauge the readiness* of the training participants. If they are unmotivated or resistant to change, this problem must be addressed. *Motivating* individuals to change involves showing them how competency training will positively affect their job performance and career in general. *Making the change self-directed* increases motivation. Participants should be assisted in choosing their own goals and designing a plan to reach them.

The goals should be *clear and manageable.* A competency can be broken down into multiple components. Its specifics must be spelled out and short- and long-term goals developed. For example, an overall goal can be to become a better communicator. It would be more productive to break down that goal into a variety of behaviors/activities involving a number of small, workable steps, such as practicing listening skills with subordinates, writing clear e-mails, and giving public presentations.

To *prevent relapse* into old habits, participants paradoxically must be prepared for slips into old behavior patterns. This enables them to learn valuable lessons and apply them to future situations. Take, for example, a manager working on self-control who, under pressure, loses his temper over a trivial matter. The manager can learn that under certain stressors he may revert to his old pattern of losing control. He can evaluate the specific triggers for this behavior and plan and practice possible alternative behaviors.

Ongoing *performance feedback* should be built into the change/action plan. This not only helps the participant to keep on track, but allows for the person to continuously modify the plan as needed. If the feedback is positive, it builds motivation and self-confidence. If negative, it alerts the participant and trainer to important information that can be used to modify the training or goals.

The key to lasting change is *practice,* both on and off the job. Again, didactic learning is only the beginning. Nor is it enough to have one or two experiential workshops or trainings, even intensive ones. Naturally arising (or planned) opportunities both inside and outside of work may be used to practice new behaviors. In a similar vein, ongoing *support* for the participant should be arranged. This may include a mentor, temporary coach, or like-minded people who are also working on competency development.

High-status, well-respected organizational leaders who exemplify the competency *provide models* who inspire change. In this regard, an organization that provides a supportive environment will *encourage* change. The competency to be developed should be consistent with organizational values, and participants should know that developing the competency will be acknowledged and rewarded. This *reinforcement of change* may take a number of forms, such as praise, increased responsibility, or financial remuneration.

Finally, Goleman recommends that a company *evaluate* the effectiveness of the training program. Objective pre- and post-training measures, plus a long-term follow-up months later, will allow a company to see if its time and money were well spent. If the training program followed most of the practices described above, chances are the company will find the program effective.

Endnotes

1 D. C. McClelland, "Testing for Competence Rather than for Intelligence," *American Psychologist* 28 (1973): 1–14.

2. D. Goleman, *Working with Emotional Intelligence* (New York: Bantam Books, 1998), 16.

3. Ibid.

4. L. M. Spencer and S. M. Spencer, *Competence at Work: Models for Superior Performance* (New York: John Wiley & Sons, Inc., 1993).

5. D. Goleman, *Emotional Intelligence: Why It Can Matter More than IQ* (New York: Bantam Books, 1995).

6. P. Salovey and J. D. Mayer. "Emotional Intelligence," *Imagination, Cognition, and Personality,* Vol. 9 (1990). Cited in Goleman, *Working with Emotional Intelligence.*

7. D. Goleman, *Working with Emotional Intelligence,* 317.

8. Ibid.

9. For a detailed description of these research methods, see Spencer and Spencer, *Competence at Work.*

10. W. C. Taylor, "Lessons for Leaders," *Fast Company,* (June 1999): 134.

11. G. J. Millman, "Visionary CFOs," *Financial Executive* (Jan/Feb 1999): 16.

12. Goleman, *Working with Emotional Intelligence,* 24.

13. Ibid., 26–27.

14. The following discussion is based on D. Goleman, "What Makes a Leader?" *Constructor* (May 1999), as well as his *Working with Emotional Intelligence.*

15. Goleman, "What Makes a Leader?" 21.

16. "Poor Communications." *Newsweek*, August 12, 1996. Cited in Goleman, *Working with Emotional Intelligence,* 175.

17. Goleman, *Working with Emotional Intelligence,* 223.

18. J. Fitz-Enz, *The Eight Practices of Exceptional Companies* (New York: American Management Association, 1997). Cited in Goleman, *Working with Emotional Intelligence,* 301.

19. Goleman, "What Makes a Leader?" 26.

20. Goleman, *Working with Emotional Intelligence,* 258–277.

Overview and Discussion
of Case Studies

Leverage Competencies and Financial Leadership

onsistent with the observations made in chapter 1, all study participants maintained that the role of financial executives has increasingly
shifted from an emphasis on conformance, command, and control to
becoming a strategic business partner. This sentiment was expressed
across the human resources (HR), business, and finance executives who
were interviewed, as exemplified by the following statements.

James Conti, HR director for finance, Unilever Home & Personal
Care-USA:

> We want to be the partner of choice.... To do that, we want to bring
> to the party not only our functional expertise, but beyond that a sig-
> nificant degree of leadership....

Mark Bye, vice president and general manager, Performance
Chemicals Division, Air Products and Chemicals, Inc.:

> Previously, the controllership function simply provided answers to
> questions posed by the team. Now, controllership is an intimate
> part of that team.

Fred Schiff, vice president, financial operations and controller,
Bristol-Myers Squibb:

> While our people have finance skills and finance backgrounds, they
> are really an integral part of our businesses...welcome participants
> at the business decision-making tables of our organization.

To be clear, many were sure to note that traditional finance skills/roles are the bedrock of being an effective financial executive. Greg Polcer, vice president finance at Unilever-HPC, described much of the role of the finance executive as that of "consigliere," an internal consultant/confidante who partners with the most senior people in the organization. He stressed, however, that finance executives must fulfill their traditional responsibilities: "Until you do that, you don't have the right to do anything else."

The role of consigliere, or strategic partner, requires proficiency in a number of "soft skills." Polcer was typical in his emphasis on the need for interpersonal skills among today's financial executives:

> The people who I am dealing with have to have faith that I have more than just a "bean counter's" mentality, that I have a real sense of the business.... Influencing skills, relationship building, leadership, team commitment [and other competencies] are all relevant to building this credibility.

Intrapersonal competencies were also emphasized across interviews. Guy Mercier, vice president, finance, Solvay Polymers (Solvay), for example, astutely discusses stress management and adaptability:

> Financial executives that don't handle stress well become rigid and intolerant to change. They increasingly retreat into what they are comfortable with and what they know already works. They are simply not prepared for an ever-changing world and certainly are in no position to partner with the businesses of an organization.

While those interviewed were provided with a list of leverage competencies (see study protocol in appendix A), they typically went beyond this list. (We emphasized that the list was simply meant to help stimulate discussion, not to offer an exhaustive or mutually exclusive list of leverage competencies.) In short, most of the emotional competencies outlined in chapter 2 came up in the interviews as being relevant to the financial executive who would be a business partner. Other, more cognitive competencies noted in chapter 2 were also discussed.

The following section reviews some of the competencies that were highlighted in the interviews. It should be noted at the outset, however, that a "Top Ten" list of leverage competencies for finance executives as a whole might be misleading. One finding was that different competency profiles may be obtained for different finance executives depending on the company and their specific position in that company. Further sections review the place of **corporate culture** in competency development, how companies are working to "make the soft stuff hard," and specific competency training practices. Common challenges will be discussed and a blueprint for incorporating leverage competencies within your organization will be outlined. The chapter concludes with a brief summary of each of the eight case studies included in this investigation.

Leverage Competencies for Financial Executives: Highlights

Most of the leverage competencies that research participants highlighted may be placed within Goleman's emotional competence framework, described in chapter 2.

Self-Awareness

Every company participating in the study understood the importance of self-awareness as a key competency, and some noted that this competency is the foundation upon which all others are built. All participating companies provide in-depth assessment using such tools as 360-degree feedback evaluations and assessment centers. Some interviewees, like Paul Huck, vice president and corporate controller, Air Products, described how self-awareness in and of itself helped finance executives to become more effective leaders.

Self-Regulation

Self-control (e.g., stress management), conscientiousness (taking responsibility for one's performance), and especially trustworthiness/ integrity were identified either directly or indirectly by a number of study participants as important for financial executives. Creating an environment of integrity and trust has been built into a number of leadership models (see, for example, Air Products, Synovus Financial Corp., and Unilever-HPC studies).

Many participants also emphasized adaptability/change management as a core competency for finance executives. Paul Huck speaks for many when he states, "The ability to champion change, embrace change, and show the troops that change is something which leads to opportunity instead of difficulty is extremely valuable." While innovation was not often directly identified, it was often tied indirectly to other competencies such as change leadership or vision. Dana Corporation (Dana) has a built-in emphasis on innovation as an integral part of the "Dana Style." Dana expects "two ideas, per person, per month, with 80 percent implementation."

Motivation

Unilever-HPC includes entrepreneurial drive as one of its 11 competencies in its Global Competency Model. This competency bears a striking resemblance to achievement drive. However, the competencies in this category were, for the most part, identified only indirectly. For example, initiative may be linked to change leadership. Commitment, aligning with the organizational goals, was discussed more as a quality to be fostered by a company than as a personal competency.

Paul Garwood, CEO of a large business unit at Unilever-HPC, believes there is an important competency that involves curiosity:

> To occupy the position I'm talking about, which is a part of a multi-functional, multiprocess team, there is a competency which is about awareness of connections, interest in, curiosity about, what's going on out there.... The breadth of perception one needs to operate effectively is getting broader. It's getting broader geographically and industrially, as boundaries start blurring and you suddenly find yourself in competition with somebody who you'd never have dreamt five years ago you'd be competing with.... "Curiosity" is linked to this greater breadth and to the ability to contribute to your team.

Curiosity drives information seeking, one of the competencies that Spencer and Spencer[1] outline, which may in turn be linked to achievement drive.

Empathy

Many interviewees emphasized the need for an awareness of the feelings, needs, and concerns of others. An important role for a leader, they maintained, is to coach or mentor their employees. Says Anne

Dawahare, former president, Synovus Technologies, Inc., "I don't really have anything I must do [more important than] keeping my people well-informed and helping them grow." William Nigh, senior vice president, also of Synovus, states, "Leadership development is my role, my responsibility." Understanding others and developing others are, of course, instrumental competencies for effective coaching/mentoring.

Service orientation was another often-highlighted competency. In fact, Nortel Networks Corporation notes that customer orientation is a given, or a "table stakes" competency. In other words, it is thought to be so basic that it was not included as one of the 12 core Finance Performance Dimensions, or competencies.

Leveraging diversity is a corporate goal for many of the companies studied, in addition to being a respected competency. Remarks Garwood, "There's no point in having diversity if you can't at least make 2 plus 2 equal 4.1. We've all seen occasions where it's added up to 3.9." Interviewees emphasized that this quality includes leveraging diversity not only in terms of culture, race, ethnicity, and gender, but also respecting diverse ways of thinking and behaving.

Social Skills

As discussed in chapter 2, the interpersonal skill competencies are the ones that are most obviously critical to effective leadership. Thus, it comes as no surprise that, aside from self-awareness, these were the ones mentioned most often by interviewees.

Communication and influencing skills are universally valued. W. L. Gore & Associates has made communication the centerpiece of its Leadership Effectiveness Training (LET) program. LET is more than a training program; it articulates a leadership model. In the halls and meeting rooms at Gore hang framed summaries of the program's key points and LET behaviors.

Conflict management, change catalyst/leadership, building bonds (relationship building), collaboration and cooperation, and team capabilities were all cited by interviewees as critical skills for finance executives who would be business partners.

Cognitive Competencies

As discussed in chapter 2, the cognitive competencies are usually thought of as "threshold competencies"—those of which leaders are expected to have some mastery. Just as Nortel Networks did not include customer orientation among the 12 Finance Performance Dimensions because it is considered a given, so too does it consider analysis a given.

Some of the executives discussed the role of strategic vision, a cognitive competency. But here too, just having vision is not enough, they pointed out.

Michael Mee, senior vice president and CFO, Bristol-Myers Squibb, said, "Vision is important but it usually comes from experience and learning how to work with the idea and the people around you."

Mark Landry, senior vice president, finance, Unilever-HPC, noted, "It is incumbent upon the CFO to breathe life into the vision...."

Thus, again, cognitive competencies may be important, but without the requisite emotional competencies, they may not be leveraged into true financial leadership.

Risk Management

Risk management is another important ability for financial executives. According to Guy Mercier of Solvay, the risk manager is not necessarily the one who actually takes the risk; that is the role of the business manager. Rather, the risk manager is the person who measures, controls, and eventually hedges the risk and has the ability to both ask and help ascertain answers to the right questions. States Mercier,

> The [finance person] is seen as risk averse.... This need not be the case, especially if [they] are viewed more as a business partner. To accomplish this, the finance person needs to be able to communicate effectively, translating risk into business and organizational objectives.

These sentiments are echoed by Mark Landry:

> The role of the CFO will be huge here...in looking for innovation, change.... A finance person can create an environment which either shuts down ideas [or] gets people to take more chances.

Leverage Competencies: Final Comments

Different competencies at different levels of mastery are required for financial executives, depending on their position. Also bearing on the most important competencies for financial executives are the goals of their organization and the corporate culture within which they operate. These will be discussed further.

Finally, consistent with the discussion of emotional competencies in chapter 2, we found that leverage competencies become more important the higher one goes in the organization. A number of the companies we studied have developed competency-based position profiles, which show that higher levels of mastery for various competencies are required at higher ranks of leadership in the organization.

Corporate Culture and Leverage Competencies

The place of leverage competencies within an organization must be understood in the context of its culture. Corporate culture and values directly and indirectly influence the role of financial executives in an organization and the nature and form of competency development among finance associates. Recall the discussion in chapter 2 on *emotionally intelligent organizations*. Such organizations display leadership characteristics similar to the ones an emotionally intelligent individual displays.

An emotionally intelligent organization has an environment that supports, if not actively promotes, leverage competencies among its people. Of course, there is an interaction between the organizational environment and its employees' leadership qualities.

An emotionally competent leader will help to create a positive, productive work environment. In turn, an emotionally intelligent work environment will attract and retain emotionally competent people.

An analysis or rating of each of the study companies in terms of their emotional intelligence is beyond the scope of this research. Many of the interviews, however, included discussions regarding the company's culture, some of which related to the concept of organizational emotional intelligence.

The study includes two companies that have been consistently named as among the "100 Best Companies to Work for in America" by *Fortune* magazine. One of these companies is Synovus Financial, which was ranked number one in the country for 1999. Founded by highly spiritual leaders, this company has fundamental values and ideals that have resulted in what has been called "a culture of the heart." Although creating shareholder value is, of course, a company priority, it is not its primary goal. It is natural for companies to promote leverage competencies as a means to an end (shareholder value), but Synovus sees people development as an end unto itself. According to its 1998 annual report, "Every decision we make, every action we take, is based on our most fundamental ideals, the beliefs that built this company. Treat people right. Do what's right. Everyone should know someone cares."

To ensure that its values would continue in the face of rapid change and growth, Synovus developed a number of structures and processes to translate its values into concrete behaviors among team members. Many of these behaviors relate directly to leverage competencies such as communication, leveraging diversity, service orientation, trustworthiness, and developing others.

Although some of these processes directly incorporate competency-based tools or mechanisms, the term "competency" is not widely used at Synovus. A Synovus executive related an anecdote in which an associate from another company heard about Synovus' performance development planning process. The associate said his company did something similar, but called it a competency evaluation performance assessment. This company, however, had difficulty implementing the program because of a lack of acceptance among its team members, who found it threatening. At Synovus, with its environment of trust and support, this system has been more readily accepted.

W. L. Gore is the study's other highly ranked "Best Company to Work for in America." Its "lattice organization" results in a company with minimal chains of command and a model of leadership defined by such terms as partnership, collaborative, participative, group-centered, and democratic. Like Synovus, Gore created a leadership model to both reflect and maintain its values and ideals. Gore's emphasis on communication is an especially important competency in such a democratic atmosphere. Such an atmosphere also fosters the role of strategic partner for finance associates.

A few other examples of the relationship between corporate culture and leverage competencies are worth noting here. Nortel Networks provides an excellent example of the interactive, reciprocal nature of corporate culture and leverage competency initiatives. The culture of Nortel Networks' finance organization supported leadership development initiatives. In turn, these initiatives fed back into the culture. This was done quite purposefully. Those who led very strong, competency-based leadership development initiatives knew that for these efforts to fully take hold, they must be woven into the established structures of the organization and into the very fabric of the culture. As one Nortel executive said, "It was a cultural sweep."

At Dana, the "Dana Style" refers to a culture that places a premium on participation and involvement. The (now former) CFO of Dana notes that "It is now the responsibility of our current chairman to inculcate that style and pass it on to the next generation of leaders...." Nurturing and maturing its leaders through specific developmental experiences, supported by careful mentoring, is a priority at the company.

Unilever-HPC presents another example of the place of corporate culture in relation to leverage competencies. In 1997, three Unilever companies with three very different corporate cultures integrated to form Unilever-HPC. Finance, while itself coping with the technical aspects of this integration, also played an important role in bringing together these disparate cultures. And Unilever-HPC's global competency model provides a common denominator for people **selection** and development at the newly integrated company.

Making the Soft Stuff Hard

Promoting and developing leverage competencies is all about making the so-called "soft stuff" or "soft skills" hard. Each of these competencies can be **operationalized,** that is, defined in terms of behaviors that are objective (to varying degrees) and measurable. The degree to which one demonstrates mastery of these abilities can then be assessed, and programs can be designed to develop key traits.

This section reviews some of the ways in which companies are working toward making the soft stuff "hard." We use the term "working toward" because everyone interviewed indicated that their companies are works in progress. The companies differ in the degree to which they employ explicit competency-based programs and processes. And some may do so, but not explicitly use the term "competencies." All, however, have created some form of assessing and developing certain desired behaviors/abilities among their people that relate to leadership. Some of these initiatives apply specifically to finance, others to the company as a whole.

Leverage competency assessment and development may be incorporated within any number of people selection and development processes. Again, the companies vary in the processes and procedures they employ. Space does not permit us to review all of them. Throughout our discussion, however, we continue to present examples obtained from our interviews.

Determining Key Leverage Competencies

The first step in leverage competency development is to identify the competencies that an organization values. These may be company-wide or relevant to a particular function, team, or a particular job or role. The companies may identify these competencies for a variety of reasons. As discussed above, some of the companies have worked to develop models specifically to operationalize their values and ideals. Others are interested in creating shareholder value by choosing and developing competencies for superior job performance. Of course, these goals are not mutually exclusive.

Gore and Synovus are companies in which leverage competencies are incorporated into leadership models that include behaviors that the corporate culture values. Gore's finance function also has its own model—Financial Services Expectations—that includes behaviors that will get finance to, and keep it at, the business decision-making table. Nortel Networks' finance function has been a leader in competency-based initiatives. In doing so, it used existing tools and processes. It identified 12 of 22 performance dimensions, the vast majority of which are leverage competencies especially relevant to finance. It also, however, developed the means by which intact (established) finance teams and individuals identify which of these aspects are relevant to their specific area.

Unilever-HPC developed a Global Competency Model that highlights a set of 11 competencies associated with superior job performance among managers. Originally introduced as a tool to identify high-potential managers, the 11 competencies are now used globally as a hiring tool as well as for career development for all manager-level employees. For professional employees (supervisor and above), Unilever-HPC uses a level system to classify jobs. The 11 competencies are the same for each work level, but the behaviors that form the competencies differ by level. Subsets of the competencies are identified as being especially relevant for different groups or individuals. As noted earlier, some companies (e.g., Bristol-Myers Squibb, Solvay) have developed specific **position profiles** that incorporate certain leverage competencies.

Air Products has a global leadership model—the Air Products Leader—that outlines specific behaviors to be modeled, capabilities to be demonstrated, and skills to be applied. The controllership function also has a competency ladder. Competencies are grouped into four categories: personal skills, leadership skills, technical skills, and functional skills. Employees and their supervisors rank employees on various behaviorally based dimensions. It is expected that an employee at a certain grade level within the function will demonstrate certain levels of competence.

Leverage Competencies and Selection
As discussed in chapter 2, it may be more cost-effective to select for certain leadership abilities than to develop them. Companies can assess leverage competencies in the hiring process. Unilever-HPC, Nortel Networks, and Air Products are among the companies that do so.

In 1998, Unilever-HPC implemented a competency-based selection system to identify people with the attributes and skills best suited for success at the company. In this process, candidates are asked questions that probe their proficiency level on several competencies that have been identified as critical to the job for which they are applying. Competency-based interviews help interviewers collect accurate behavioral information about job candidates, which is used to evaluate the candidate and determine whether to offer the job.

Recently, finance at Unilever-HPC hired a group of assistant commercial managers from Masters of Business Administration (MBA) programs across the United States. Six competencies were identified as key for the assistant commercial manager position. An interview protocol was created for this position that included questions designed to determine the skill level for each of the six competencies. Interviewers are provided with specific questions to ask for each competency, which they follow up with probing questions. Each question seeks specific behavioral examples of a candidate's past job performance.

Scoring standards are determined in advance, and the interviewers use them to assess the candidate's responses to each question. In many cases, panel interviews occur so that more than one person can rate a candidate's answers. All employees who conduct interviews go through extensive training in the competency-based interviewing approach.

Nortel Networks uses **behavioral event job interviews.** Specific guides have been developed based on a Performance Dimensions Dictionary. Key performance dimensions and mastery levels needed for success in a given job in finance are outlined. Further, the performance dimensions are listed in the job profile, so a job candidate can consider whether he or she is a good fit for the role and anticipate what questions an interviewer might ask.

At Air Products, MBA job candidates for finance go through an assessment center that includes the evaluation of a variety of personal competencies through job simulation exercises and interviews. The competency categories include leading and influencing, communication and interpersonal skills, problem solving and creativity, and teamwork.

Some procedures that are not meant specifically to evaluate leadership may still have the effect of promoting behaviors important to a company. For example, Synovus' hiring process, while not specifically competency based, is extensive. As many as 15 job interviews are not unheard of at this company. At these interviews, interviewers get to know a candidate and his or her values, and the candidate gets to know the company's values. Such a process may facilitate a match between the company and individuals who will ultimately demonstrate qualities consistent with the company's culture.

Linking Leverage Competencies to Organizational Goals

Most of the executives interviewed noted that competency identification and development should not occur in a vacuum. They must relate to and facilitate organizational goals. Thus, in many companies, employees create personal goals, including competency development, that take into account team, function, and/or corporate goals and priorities.

Finance at Nortel Networks developed a specific initiative to align business objectives with the roles and competencies of team members. This initiative is called Objective Alignment. In this process, objectives cascade from the CEO to the CFO and business president to finance teams, and ultimately, individuals. The objectives are SMART—specific, measurable, actionable, realistic, and time bound. (Interestingly, Unilever-HPC similarly uses the SMART acronym for target setting—stretch, measurable, achievable, relevant, and timeframed.)

Some companies tied specific behaviors or competencies to **critical success factors,** which were then related to business objectives. In fact, this is the crux of Gore's Financial Leadership Model, which involves identifying performance metrics that will best promote the behaviors leading to critical success factors (securing a place at the business decision-making table), which then lead to satisfying the purposes of the business (enhancing shareholder value).

Performance Review/Development Planning

It is the norm that every employee goes through **performance reviews and development planning.** This is, of course, a logical place to include planning for leverage competency development. Everyone interviewed agreed that continuous dialogue between employees and managers is the cornerstone of development planning. What the process does, however, is provide a formal structure, operationalizing as much as possible performance reviews and development planning.

Some of the companies have formal, competency-based performance evaluation and development processes. Unilever-HPC's performance assessment and development system—Performance Development Planning (PDP)—aligns personal development goals with organizational ones and provides ongoing feedback about needed skills and competencies. Included in this process is an assessment of the Unilever-HPC competencies by both manager and employee and creation of specific Competency Development Plans.

Nortel Networks also has a competency-based performance assessment and development system emphasizing continuous dialogue between manager and employee. It reviews both results and the way those results are achieved—that is, through competencies. It does so by using Performance Dimensions. Again, both manager and employee assess the relevant competencies and plan ways to develop them.

The Air Products controllership function uses the competency ladder in its performance appraisal and development system. Synovus' Right Steps is described as "a continuous performance development planning process. It is a shift in emphasis from evaluation and judgment toward coaching and development." Like the others mentioned, it includes at least one major skill or competency to be developed and establishes specific measures to monitor progress.

Companies such as Bristol-Myers Squibb and Solvay use position profiles, including various competencies, in their performance development process. Bristol-Myers' performance development processes include Performance Partnerships and the Career Dialogue. These processes involve employees communicating their career aspirations to their managers, identifying the standards of performance as embodied in the online position profiles, and seeking feedback and coaching to identify experiences that will help them develop and work toward their goals.

Human Resource/Succession Planning
Companies often have mechanisms for long-term career development planning for some or all of their people. The mechanisms may involve ways to identify and develop **"high potentials,"** individuals viewed as a company's future stars or leaders. A competency-based system may be useful here, too.

Nortel Networks' finance function has Career Development Readiness Reviews for all finance employees. This process looks at each employee's readiness for a development move. Before competency-based processes were initiated, these reviews were viewed by many as too subjective and secretive. Now, competency-based data are incorporated into the decision-making process.

Unilever-HPC's Human Resources Planning Process (HRPP) includes the identification of employees with high potential, a discussion and review of individual development plans, and **succession planning.** Information from its Performance Development Planning System, including competency assessments, feeds into this process. Employees are rated against both job skills and leverage competencies to see if they are performing at or above the expected levels for their job. In turn, succession planning and nominations for specialized training that result from the HRPP become input for follow-up PDP career discussions.

While not leverage competency-based, Dana's emphasis on experiential learning, promoting from within, and maturity is reflected in its "obsession" with succession planning. Says Dana's (now former) CFO, "One thing that we cherish at Dana—it's almost sacrosanct—is our leadership succession program." This program involves intensive selection meetings. Once these potential leaders are identified, they become part of an extensive cross-functional mentoring program. For example, the CFO might be mentoring one of the next presidents of foreign operations, while the current president of the automotive systems group might be mentoring the next CFO.

Leverage Competency Training Practices

There is an extensive array of formal and informal training opportunities to develop leverage competencies. Some companies, such as Unilever-HPC and Nortel Networks, directly provide information to their people regarding competency development. Unilever-HPC's intranet-based Learning Resource Center includes information and suggestions about a wide variety of methods and opportunities to develop each of its 11 competencies. Nortel's Performance Dimensions Development Map includes recommendations for developing each performance dimension.

In general, the opportunities for developing leverage competencies include internal or external structured learning/workshops, coaching/ mentoring, and any number of experiential development opportunities. While they are taken separately, there is much overlap in these training and development methods. In fact, the most intensive competency training programs carefully integrate all of these development opportunities.

Structured Learning/Workshops

Almost everyone interviewed reported that their companies had some form of coursework or workshops relating to various leverage competencies. Each year at Dana, two to three thousand employees attend programs offered by Dana University. Those who are interested can even earn a fully accredited MBA or MS degree in engineering. Dana University offers a Manager Certification Program, which includes training in leverage competencies through such courses as How to Develop Your Personal Strengths for Effective Managing.

Air Products has five intensive Leadership Education Modules and offers a variety of in-house corporate training courses pertaining to a number of competencies. Synovus too offers hundreds of in-house training courses, such as Effective Communication and Power Coaching. It also has the Leadership Institute, which provides intensive leadership training through three progressively advanced leadership programs. The programs range from one to two years in length and include assessments, personal development planning, classroom instruction, business simulations, and community-based and on-the-job learning projects designed to help leaders integrate new behaviors and skills in the workplace.

Nortel launched its competency-based initiatives through intensive Mapping Your Future (MYF) workshops. They involved aligning business objectives with role performance dimensions and assessing personal strengths and weaknesses against those performance dimensions. The outcome was a detailed competency-based people development plan for each finance department. This workshop will not be routinely repeated. Since the model was established, it (and its supporting tools and materials) has been integrated into various structures. All new hires will work with their managers on role definitions, competencies, and developing competency-based growth plans.

Many of the companies offer external training at outside universities, training organizations, and so forth. Most prefer, however, to have internally based training, preferably facilitated by the company's employees. This is because companies want training to be integrated within their own corporate culture and structures. As will be discussed below, a number of those interviewed stressed that training should be a process, not an event. This brings us to other, more ongoing methods of competency development.

Mentoring/Coaching
Many companies offer professional executive coaching, which involves working one on one with a trained executive coach. The coaching process usually involves an extensive assessment, including a 360-degree feedback evaluation. The coach then develops a focused program emphasizing behavior (and where appropriate, attitude) change. Leverage competency development may or may not be a focus of coaching. Coaching may be a one-time experience (although all usually offer some form of follow-up) or ongoing as needed.

Most of the companies we studied, however, while offering professional coaching, emphasize a more internally based, continuous coaching or mentoring process. All emphasize the importance of continuous dialogue between employees and managers to each employee's (and often manager's) professional growth and development—competency-based or otherwise. Some companies, like Synovus, would like every manager to be a mentor.

Dana's cross-functional mentoring program was already noted in the context of succession planning. Solvay also has an extensive mentoring program. At Solvay, a mentor is not an individual's supervisor or even someone from the same department. A mentor is someone who has gone through the company's mentoring program and from whom an employee can freely seek advice and direction.

At Gore, every associate must have a **sponsor** from the very beginning of his or her career. Initially they are assigned, but each associate is free to change sponsors. Again, the sponsor of a financial associate may not be from finance. The role of sponsors is taken very seriously. They are responsible for the performance and development process of each sponsored associate. For finance associates, sponsors are asked to assess their people against Financial Services Expectations, mentioned earlier. The associate looks to the sponsor for feedback, behavioral guidance, and access to team-based work experiences that will broaden the associate's ability to contribute to the organization.

Experiential Development

All of the companies that participated in this study would agree with Goleman's emphasis, discussed in chapter 2, on experience for the development of leverage competencies. Experience is, in fact, the *sine qua non* of leverage competency development. Coursework, workshops, coaching, and mentoring must ultimately be tied to the real work world.

We feel that a Synovus executive spoke for everyone interviewed in our study when he stated that leadership development cannot be just an event:

> While important, [formal leadership] training courses are events. I go, and I'm charged up, and it might change me for a week. In two weeks, I've got 50 percent of it, and in three weeks nobody ever knew I went.

The Synovus Leadership Institute incorporates both community and job-based experiences as part of a participant's personalized development plan. In fact, all of the companies stress personal development through experience. Some of these experiences are planned specifically for the purpose of developing various leverage competencies. Some may not use the term "competencies," but specific behaviors and competencies are targeted nonetheless. Others are more for the purpose of grooming or maturing an individual, thus indirectly developing leverage competencies.

Most programs include an assessment procedure to evaluate competencies in need of development. Then, in concert with a trainer, supervisor, and/or mentor, experiences are designed to help the individual work on those skills. Some of these experiences may be very focused. For example, an individual development plan might include giving three public presentations over the next six months to complement communication training. Other experiences may be much broader, such as leading a cross-functional team or volunteering financial services to a community program in an inner-city neighborhood. These experiences are often supervised and done in conjunction with other development opportunities such as coaching or coursework.

The finance function of many of the study companies allows, if not requires, its people to have cross-functional experiences. At Bristol-Myers Squibb, for example, finance people transfer throughout the organization more than employees from any other function. Its entry-level MBA program includes business rotations that provide new finance associates with a variety of business experiences. Says one executive at Bristol-Myers,

> We believe that experience is the greatest teacher, so moving people into new roles, with new opportunities for learning, is the best way to aid in their business development.

Interacting with others in the business may facilitate leverage competency development in and of itself. Mark Bye, a business executive at Air Products, remarked that finance people who have been acting as business partners have grown through their relationships with nonfinance people:

There is a lot to be gained by being exposed to different personalities and cultures. For example, the classic field representative is different from the classic accountant. Both have benefited from interactions. They've discovered parts of their personalities that they were reluctant to let out, didn't seem acceptable, etc., and there have been some changes in behavior—they express themselves differently than they would have not so long ago. So experience itself has spurred the development of competencies.

Challenges

Unilever-HPC has in place sophisticated, comprehensive, competency-based people selection and development processes. Jim Conti, HR director for finance, is far from complacent, however. He states that a challenge for the organization is to truly make this a part of the corporate culture:

> How do we institutionalize these behaviors? How do we make them known in such a way that people say, "I need these things to be a leader. How do I put them into everyday practice. How do I develop them?" We continue to work on this.

This is just one of many challenges companies must face in their attempts to use and develop leverage competencies throughout the organization, including finance. As stated earlier, every study company viewed leverage competency development as a work in progress. Like any people initiatives, competency development can be challenging.

Lack of Acceptance

Acceptance of competency-based initiatives at all levels of the company can be difficult to achieve. Assessing competencies and insisting on their development can be threatening, especially if an individual's success has been predicated on more traditional or technical skills. A finance executive who graduated from a top school and worked hard at becoming highly skilled in a variety of traditional finance skills may not appreciate suddenly hearing that the rules have changed.

Recall the story recounted by the Synovus executive about an associate whose prior company had a competency evaluation performance assessment program. This program had difficulty taking hold because employees did not accept it. Synovus may not routinely use the term "competencies," but it makes a concerted effort to create an environment that values and rewards their development.

Different Attitudes Regarding the Role of Finance
In a similar vein, while the trend in finance is to embrace the role of finance associate as strategic business partner, that may not be universal in the organization. For example, Unilever-HPC was the result of an integration of three Unilever companies with very different cultures. Part of the cultural differences included the extent to which finance was viewed by itself and others more traditionally instead of in the strategic partner role.

Deeply Integrating Leverage Competencies
Conti of Unilever-HPC hopes to institutionalize leverage competency behaviors, to make them a part of everyday practice. It is all too easy to make them an event or series of events. While competency- or behavior-based structures and processes go a long way toward institutionalizing leverage competencies, they must be embraced by manager and employee, made relevant, and frequently discussed at all levels of the organization. Otherwise, little more than lip service may be given to them.

A Blueprint for Facilitating Leverage Competencies in Your Organization

Given our findings, and the work of Goleman and others described in chapter 2, we offer a list of recommendations for integrating, selecting for, and developing leverage competencies in your organization. It is not meant to be definitive or exhaustive. The needs and values of your particular organization will dictate the place of leverage competencies and competency development.

- *Gain the support of major stakeholders.* Many of those interviewed attributed their success in implementing competency-based people processes to having the support of stakeholders at all levels.

Active support from the highest levels of the organization should be frequently communicated.

■ *Make the programs consistent with corporate values.* Initiatives will flow more easily from values that are widely held throughout the corporation.

■ *Make leverage competencies and leverage competency development in others relevant and rewarded.* Organization members should see the relevance of leverage competencies for their job and career. They should be rewarded for exhibiting these competencies with salary increases, bonuses, and promotions. Similarly, leaders should be rewarded for developing leverage competencies in others.

■ *Determine which leverage competencies are the most relevant to your organization, function, and job.* Ideally, a company should assess which competencies are important not only to finance, but to each team and team member.

■ *Align leverage competencies with corporate/business goals.* Development of leverage competencies should not be done in a vacuum.

■ *Make the soft stuff hard.* Leverage competencies have traditionally been thought of as soft—vague, subjective and difficult to pin down, assess, or develop. The technology now exists to make them more objective, concrete, and measurable.

■ *Provide thorough individual assessment and feedback.* Through such means as 360-degree feedback and assessment centers, individuals can be evaluated on their strengths and developmental needs for leverage competencies. Feedback should be given, of course, in a sensitive, supportive manner to help motivate those individuals.

■ *Incorporate leverage competencies into employee selection and development structures.* Competency-based processes and procedures can be incorporated into every phase of the people selection and development processes. Selecting for leverage competencies may be just as important as developing them.

- *Make leverage competency development a continuous process.* Development of leverage competencies is not an event, it is a career-long process. Manager and employee should maintain a continuous dialogue regarding leverage competency development.

- *Emphasize experience.* Experience is the *sine qua non* of leverage competency development. No one will ever master a leverage competency by reading a book. A wide variety of competency development opportunities exists. The most effective ones are based on experience. It may be helpful, however, to coordinate/integrate a number of training modalities. For example, coursework can lay the foundation of knowledge critical for the development of leverage competencies. Experiences designed to put this knowledge into action can be coordinated with this coursework. This experience can then be supervised and supported by a mentor with whom the associate has developed a personal competency development plan.

Overview of Case Studies by Company

Air Products and Chemicals, Inc.

The controllership function of Air Products initiated a major reorganization called Controllership 2000, or C2K. One of the primary goals of this initiative is to enhance the role of finance as strategic business partner. This vision of controllership and the place of leverage competencies as they relate to it is a primary focus of this case study.

Important insights into the strategic role of finance were offered by one of the company's top business executives. This executive appreciates the importance of leverage competencies and has seen finance people grow through these behaviors. A former expatriate, he emphasized an openness to diversity as an especially critical skill. Finally, the vice president of HR discussed leverage competencies and their development at Air Products, and important leadership initiatives that the company has established.

Bristol-Myers Squibb Company

The approach to leadership and competency development at Bristol-Myers Squibb is all-pervasive. According to the company's chairman, "everyone is expected to be a leader." Thus, the company has put into place an extensive leadership development effort that affects all employees. Much of this effort is summed up in the company's leadership model, which brings together functional skills, leadership behaviors, and "capacity"—the knowledge and experiences one possesses. To facilitate leadership and leadership development, the company has also devoted extensive resources to the development of in-house leadership courses—through its Center for Leadership Development—as well as bringing online everything from position profiles to leadership support tools.

Regarding the specific leadership development of its finance executives, the HR department works closely with senior finance executives to identify the company's future leaders. In developing leadership behaviors and competencies, experiential learning is fundamental to the company's approach. In addition, the company places a great deal of emphasis on succession planning, ensuring that its senior finance executives have ample opportunities to both identify and personally know the talent in the organization. In developing its finance people, Bristol-Myers Squibb makes no distinctions concerning requisite behaviors or expectations. From the online position profiles of the company one can readily see the emphasis on progressing from skills to behaviors as finance executives move toward higher levels of leadership responsibility.

Dana Corporation

The leadership challenge for Dana Corporation was articulated in 1990 by the company's chairman. The initiative, labeled Dana 2000, was one of the first of its kind to focus on the leadership challenges of the new millennium. Much of the company's approach to leadership is today embodied in what the company calls the Dana Style, which incorporates its approach to leadership into the very fabric and culture of the company.

For finance executives at Dana, leadership development is facilitated through the combination of hiring practices, experiential learning, succession planning, and educational support—on both the skill and behavioral fronts—through Dana University. Unlike other companies in this study that explicitly focus on competencies, Dana's approach has been more implicit and is seen as part of the normal developmental process of individuals. The Dana case incorporates the views of a wide array of individuals, ranging from the former CFO to the training staff of Dana University. Of special interest is the interview with the head of the company's audit staff, who described some of the criteria the group looks for in hiring at the entry level.

Nortel Networks Corporation

A few years ago, the current CFO of Nortel Networks called for an initiative to promote leadership development among finance employees. This request reflects a commitment at the highest levels of finance to develop its people, as well as finance's strategic role within the organization. The result was an award-winning competency-based people development initiative called Mapping Your Future (MYF).

Complementing MYF is Objective Alignment, another finance initiative, rolled out to strengthen the connection between business objectives and roles and competencies of team members. The Finance People Movement, through a number of creative programs, has made great strides in bringing the importance of competencies and their development to the forefront of finance people's consciousness. At Nortel Networks, competencies are now quantified and measured. People selection, career planning, and performance review and development processes have all become competency-based.

Solvay Polymers, Inc.

Solvay Polymers is the 100 percent owned subsidiary of Solvay, the Brussels-based global chemicals and pharmaceuticals giant. At Solvay Polymers, the approach to leadership is directly tied to attaining the crucial success factors for competitiveness, customer satisfaction, and continuous improvement. For the finance executive at Solvay Polymers, much of the leadership challenge and development focus is on ensuring the integration of finance into the company's business and decision-making processes.

What makes this case especially interesting and somewhat unique are the powerful views of the company's vice president of finance. These views bring a truly international perspective to the study.

Moreover, they present competencies in a clear manner that can be related to both the personal and business lives of finance executives.

Synovus Financial Corp.

In 1999, *Fortune* magazine selected Synovus as the "Best Company to Work for in America." The traditional, people-oriented values and ideals of this company have resulted in what has been called "a culture of the heart." Interviews with a number of leaders at Synovus offered insights into the critical position of corporate culture as it relates to leverage competencies in the organization.

The soft stuff is paramount at Synovus. The company has endeavored to create metrics for it by defining the components and behaviors that make up and support its values and leadership expectations. Synovus makes it a priority for every leader of the company to practice, teach, and facilitate those behaviors among team members. Synovus' performance development planning process incorporates leverage competencies. All managers and supervisors participate in Foundations of Leadership, a four-month program that focuses on Synovus' Leadership Expectations. The Leadership Institute offers more advanced leadership training for leaders who range from "up and coming" to presidents and CEOs. Action-based training is emphasized, including community service as well as on-the-job projects designed to develop leadership ability.

Unilever-HPC

Competencies are the foundation of employee selection and development systems at Unilever-HPC. In 1994, Unilever introduced a global competency model. Originally introduced as a tool to identify high-potential managers, its 11 competencies are now also used globally for selection, performance planning, and career planning and development for all manager-level employees.

Unilever-HPC was formed in 1997 through a merger of three Unilever companies. The implications of this merger of three very different finance cultures and the place of leverage competencies adds another dimension to this case study. In addition to interviews with the company's most senior finance executives and the vice president for HR in finance, the head of one of the companies' largest businesses was interviewed. A British national with global experience, he offered some interesting insights into the role of finance as business partner and the role of leverage competencies.

W. L. Gore & Associates, Inc.

As a participant in past Research Foundation studies on the changing roles and responsibilities of finance, Gore represents a special addition to the current study. The company also has been selected year after year as one of the best companies to work for in America by *Fortune* magazine. Gore's culture is quite unusual. There is no hierarchy of command and no job titles. The company's emphasis is on teamwork and instilling the values and behaviors that facilitate a close working relationship among all its associates. Leaders tend to emerge naturally from this process, rather than through a formal process of promotion and succession.

On the finance front, the company has instituted the global financial leadership team. Composed of only five individuals, the team has sought to raise the level of what Gore's businesses can expect from its finance professionals. With a heavy emphasis on the right behaviors, finance's goal is to add value to the company's businesses, helping it to identify its critical success factors and the metrics that will facilitate them in the most meaningful way. Given the fact that Gore's finance people are largely located at the plants, this ability to participate and influence the businesses becomes the essence of leadership. As succinctly put by one of the company's key finance leaders, "our goal is to be invited to sit at the decision-making tables of this company and help influence those business decisions that will add the greatest value for our shareholders." As the case study illustrates, from formal programs on leadership development—Leadership Effective Training—to extensive articulation of requisite behaviors, Gore's finance and HR professionals are moving rapidly to identify the competencies necessary for finance executive leadership in the future.

Endnote

1. Spencer and Spencer, *Competence at Work.* See chapter 2 for a discussion of their work.

Air Products and Chemicals, Inc.

Each of us must be willing to turn our back on business as usual...including how we look at our businesses and how we plan, budget, and report on our businesses. We must focus less of our efforts on explaining our past and more on creating our future....

John Paul Jones III, president and chief operating officer

Company Background

Its 1998 annual report describes Air Products and Chemicals, Inc., as follows:

Air Products and Chemicals, Inc. (NYSE: APD) is an international supplier of industrial gases and related equipment and specialty and intermediate chemicals. Our 17,000 employees working at operations in over 30 countries are committed to building lasting commercial relationships based on understanding our customers' businesses. And through this understanding, we continually find ways to help them win in markets around the world—while maintaining our focus on being an industry leader in safety, health, and preservation of the environment. We are headquartered in Pennsylvania's Lehigh Valley and have sales of more than $5 billion to 115 countries around the world.[1]

The controllership function of Air Products is the largest function in finance. There are approximately 450 people in the North American controllership organization. Recently, Paul Huck, vice president and corporate controller, initiated a major reorganization of the controllership function, called Controllership 2000 (C2K). One of the primary goals of this reorganization is to facilitate the role of finance as a strategic partner to the business. Huck articulated this vision of controllership and discussed leverage competencies as they relate to its realization. Thus, a major focus of this chapter will be on the controllership function.

Also interviewed was Mark Bye, vice president and general manager, Performance Chemicals division. Bye is responsible for a $1 billion global division. Performance Chemicals has approximately 14,000 customers and 2,000 products, with half of its sales outside of the United States. Bye offered important insights into the strategic role of finance, and controllership in particular, from the perspective of a business manager. He discussed his opinions regarding the importance of leverage competencies as they relate to the role of finance associates in his organization.

Finally, Joseph (Jay) McAndrew, vice president, HR, discussed his views on leverage competencies and how Air Products is addressing these competencies and leadership development in general. He, too, noted the strategic place of finance at Air Products.

Financial Leadership at Air Products: A Control Perspective

Paul Huck sums up his view of a good financial executive: "A good financial executive has a lot of the qualities that make a good business executive. Because that's what you want them to be. You are not a good business partner unless you're good at that."

Being a good business partner is at the center of Huck's vision for his function. This has been the trend for finance, and structural changes currently being implemented in controllership, discussed below, will only increase finance's strategic place within the organization.

He described a number of qualities and competencies that make a good finance/business executive:

- *Thinking both strategically and tactically.* "An executive needs to be able to not only think strategically, but also have the ability to implement strategy—to know how to make things work."

- *Providing sound judgment.* "I look for good, sound judgment, good common sense. At times the numbers tell you one thing but your gut tells you another. Numbers are only one element. I always bet on my gut."

- *Producing results.* "You have to operate in two dimensions. It's not just producing results, but how you go about doing that. For example, some people produce results by wearing people out, by beating down the organization. And when you get into some project modes, when you're fighting a battle, those people can be valuable. But when you are fighting a whole war, you don't want to give up your army or navy in the first battle. So someone who can manage execution, get the right people on the job, motivate those people, point them in the right direction, and give them the vision can operate successfully in both the short and long term."

- *Coaching others.* "An effective financial executive—someone who is a business partner—has the ability to coach people. Not just coaching people you manage, but the chief executive officer, chief operating officer, operation division heads, etc. No one knows it all. Being able to say, 'You really need to pay attention to that,' and to offer feedback and coaching to such individuals without them taking affront is extremely important, and a valuable skill when you're looking for someone who can be a partner."

- *Championing change.* "The ability to champion change, embrace change, and show the troops that change is something that leads to opportunity instead of difficulty is extremely valuable."

- *Adapting to change.* "In a changing world, in a world that is different as you go more global, etc., adaptability is important. As some of your old solutions and behaviors no longer work, you need to adapt your behavior. [Leveraging] diversity—diverse people, cultures, ways of thinking—has also become more important."

- *Communicating effectively.* "Being able to communicate effectively with a variety of people, to reach out to them in different ways, is critical. Communication is important in simply trying to motivate others and get things done. And it's important in both ways. That is, one needs to also be an effective listener, to have others know that they are being listened to and understood."

Huck also notes that, with the onset of C2K, which facilitates strategic partnering with business, these and other related competencies will grow in importance.

C2K

As mentioned above, the controllership function is in the process of being significantly and strategically restructured. According to Huck, the C2K initiatives are being driven in the pursuit of three basic goals:

1. Improving the service to the businesses

2. Improving controls within the businesses

3. Lowering cost

Previously, all controllership accountants were decentralized across the various business units, performing a variety of accounting, operations, reporting, analytical, and support functions. They performed similar processes, but as the controller noted, "not identical and not driven toward efficiency." Controllership decided to consolidate the accounting, operations, and reporting areas by creating a centralized service center that will provide these financial services to the businesses for negotiable costs.

This and other C2K initiatives free the business controllers of tasks that take time away from their primary function—to be strategic business partners:

Previously, the business controllers worried about everything. They worried about accounting, reporting, getting the bills paid, etc. We're relieving them of that. We're saying, your job is to work with the business people to make the business better. The mission of controllership is to support the success of our businesses. Ultimately, we do that by integrating business teams—totally devoting certain people in the controllership to spend 100 percent of their time making the business better.

C2K initiatives involve not only structural changes, but changes in attitudes and priorities as well. Echoing the strategic, future-oriented directive articulated by the chief operating officer (COO), Huck states,

We are working toward changing the focus of the way we look at the business. Traditionally, much of our understanding and interacting with the business revolved around the historical aspect of it. How did we perform last month? What's our performance against last year? Can I explain this? While this may be important, I would like to change the focus from a reactive, historical one to a proactive one: What am I doing to make things better? What am I doing to achieve my strategic goals? What should we be measuring? I expect the business support people to sit down and work with the operating people. My concept of the decision support person is that he/she is the assistant general manager for the business which he/she supports. To a great extent, some of our more successful people over the years have done that. Now, to be successful, you must do it. We're trying to help people with this.

To facilitate the success of these changes, workshops will be conducted to educate people about what they will and will not be doing in their new roles. Further, controllership associates will be encouraged to gain experience across all controllership functions (transaction processing; accounting, operations, and reporting; and decision support). Competencies relevant to being a good business partner may, at one time or another, be important to everyone in the controllership function.

Thus, C2K initiatives will increase the significance of leverage competencies for most, if not all, controllership associates. In discussing these, Huck adds some competencies to the list outlined above. He emphasizes that influence is a critical competency for the finance executive who would be a business partner. "For decision support, those who cannot influence are going to be useless." He also maintains that relationship building, interpersonal understanding, and working with people of different backgrounds are now especially important, given that "One of the things we are doing is forcing new relationships upon people. How you build and manage relationships becomes more important." He notes that even those not currently in decision support may need such competencies. For example, those in the service center will be negotiating agreements, and in a sense, serving as consultants. Competencies such as negotiation skills and conflict management are expected to be useful here.

4

Controllership on Competency Development

The controller is supportive of competency development for his people. He notes that the first step is assessment, and that self-awareness is an important competency in its own right. He went through a 360-degree feedback assessment himself. Through it, he gained insight into areas he could work on, and he feels he has made improvements in those areas. For example, he came from a background where the work ethic was such that you neither expected to be overtly thanked nor to praise others for simply doing their job. After receiving some feedback on this, he realized that for many, positive feedback was appropriate and important.

Huck believes that sometimes people are limited in how much they can change, and that this is a function of motivation and skill. He feels that some competencies may be more difficult to improve than others: "You may not turn a person into the greatest communicator of all time, but you can certainly make him or her a lot better. Other competencies, such as adaptability, aren't so much skills as they are qualities, and may be more difficult to develop."

He stated that MBA job candidates for finance go through an assessment center, which involves evaluating a variety of personal competencies through job simulation exercises and interviews. The competency categories examined include leading and influencing, communication and interpersonal skills, problem solving and creativity, and teamwork. Thus, the hiring process itself preselects for many competencies. Since some competencies may indeed be more difficult than others to develop, this is a valuable process.

Regarding competency development, controllership has a competency ladder as part of its performance review/enhancement process. It involves having both employee and supervisor evaluate the employee against various competencies, both technical and personal. The development of some of these competencies may then be included in an employee's career development plan. HR offers courses on the development of leverage competencies. Huck notes, however, that "The problem we have there is making sure managers know it's out there and to have them utilize it. We probably haven't paid as much attention as we need to for some of the future skills which people need. As the needs of the company change, we're going to have to provide opportunities to change—in terms of both technical and soft skills."

The competency ladder and courses developed by HR are discussed below.

Financial Leadership at Air Products: A Business Perspective

Mark Bye's vision of what makes a good financial executive mirrors that of the controller. He expects his finance associates to be valued strategic partners. He notes that this has been an important, welcome trend over the past few years, to the point that "If someone today would use the term 'bean counter' in describing finance people, they would be seen as a dinosaur. That moniker is totally a thing of the past." Like the controller, he sees the C2K initiatives as playing an important part in making this happen.

He, too, emphasized the need for a more future-oriented, proactive focus: "We've spent a disproportionate time historically accounting for decisions which have already been made as opposed to focusing on strategic, proactive analysis." He notes that with the increasing complexity of the business and greater access to knowledge systems and data, prioritization has become critical. Finance plays an important role in this process:

> A critical input into that prioritization process is looking at the financial data in a way that is less driven by accounting accuracy than it is by looking at what fundamental trends emerge. There may be some things not obvious to the nonfinancially trained eye that are relevant and may be important drivers for a key decision, such as raising a price, where we first introduce a new product, where we add resources, etc. Controllership adds tremendous value in terms of sorting that out. So they've really become part of the strategic team to look at making both short-term operational and longer-term strategic decisions for us. Previously, the controllership function simply provided answers to questions posed by the team. Now, controllership is an intimate part of that team.

Given the more strategic role of finance, Bye, like Huck, recognizes the increased importance of interpersonal competencies for financial associates. Influence skills are especially important as finance people interact more with both the business and external customers:

> You can relate influence to a lot of other skills and abilities, such as interpersonal skills, working effectively in a team environment, developing personal credibility. One must balance assertiveness and confidence in one's position with listening skills and understanding the needs of others.... More and more we have finance people who are interfacing directly with customers, working together with them to design "win-win" deals. So the interpersonal skills and ability to deal effectively externally is something that's becoming very important.

Bye commented that an important shift has taken place. Historically, the traditional role of finance created a "good-soldier mentality." That is, finance was informed of changes and expected to accommodate those changes. "As we head more toward teams, the ability to go beyond just simply deciding how to respond and providing real input into the change process itself becomes more critical. That creates a shift from one core skill—adaptability—to another, which is change leadership. Adaptability will always be important, but it's less important than it was before. In fact, blind adaptability is a negative in today's world."

On a similar note, Bye points out that one important overall skill is the ability to eliminate work—to be efficient and prioritize. In doing so, one must have the ability to diplomatically say no. He commented that historically, controllership had difficulty saying no because it was not aware of the business strategy and did not have the breadth of understanding to question changes. Now that the finance function is seen as part of the strategic business team, it can more credibly question things and say no.

> The good-soldier mentality is changing. It is transitioning from reacting to what management wants to what our stakeholders need.... It used to be that whether the division had a good year or a bad year mattered less than accurately accounting for [it]. Now, it's not that way. My controller feels a part of setting our course. Are we

winning or losing? How do we know? If we're not winning, he's as upset about it as I am.

When the company is recruiting new employees, the high-potential financial candidates tend to find the more strategic, business-oriented role of finance very attractive, Bye reports.

Even among staunch finance candidates, I see an increasing desire to have either rotational assignments or some kind of experience outside of the controllership function within the business area because they are convinced it is very difficult to get to the most senior levels of finance without knowing the nuts and bolts of how businesses really operate. "Can Air Products provide that for me or am I relegated to a career within a narrow silo?" We have a Career Development Program (CDP) which gives them these opportunities. A number of graduate students are eligible for it, including MBAs. The CDP is designed to cut across historic silos. You can join the company in the finance area and take a second assignment in marketing—without the political stigma you so often find. Typically, but not always, you return to finance. They have this as an option. This is attractive to high-potential candidates. Plus, they *see* that finance is involved in strategy and development. They are excited about that.

Thus, the evolving nature of finance at Air Products should continue with a positive cycle of attracting strong finance candidates who are committed to contributing to the company's overall strategy. This should further strengthen finance and perhaps the company as a whole, attracting even stronger finance candidates.

Business on Competency Development

According to Bye, "We have courses, both internal and external, for virtually anything on your [competency] list. I think it's important that controllership goes through those courses together with other non-finance professionals so that they share experiences, strengthen relationships outside of their function, form bonds, etc. The more forums we provide to make those kinds of connections, the better off we'll be. A lot of people will learn from each other."

This highlights another important avenue to building competencies—experience. Interacting more with other functions and customers, and taking more of a leadership role, can build competencies in and of itself:

> In general, I have seen growth. Some of it is confidence to step out of the box. In the past two to three years I've seen a significant change in the nature of the proactive discussions and comments of finance people, and more comfort in being involved in this [strategic] role.... A lot too is being exposed to different personalities and cultures. For example, the classic field representative is different from the classic accountant. Both have benefited from interactions. They've discovered parts of their personalities that they were reluctant to let out, didn't seem acceptable, etc., and there have been some changes in behavior—they express themselves differently than they would have not so long ago. So experience itself has spurred the development of competencies.

Bye notes, however, that it might be helpful for experience to be augmented by training. For example, with respect to working on teams, he says, "We often have rotating leadership. We're looking for diversity within the team—styles, backgrounds, etc. How do you do that? How do you look at forming the team? Who should be on it? It would be helpful to provide training for that."

Leveraging Diversity

Mark Bye spent almost six years in Europe for Air Products. International experience gave him an appreciation for diversity issues, and, he believes, helped him acquire important competencies:

> I learned a lot during my time abroad. The value you pick up from that experience allows you to be better at a number of things in the company. Part of that is just acknowledging that there are different routes to get to the same answer that are equally valid—from how you raise a price to how you negotiate with a raw material supplier to how you motivate employees. In our acquisitions, we've benefited far more when we've looked at the organization we've just acquired to determine what we should be learning from them instead of analyzing how we need to change them to look more like us.

There may be certain practical changes [in this direction], such as accounting and reporting standards. But there's a number of other areas where we have tremendous learning opportunities from the companies we've acquired or interfaced with.

One of my biggest rewards from my international assignment was learning to listen. I used to be skilled at explaining to someone why my way—or the Air Products way—was the best way. This can be an important skill if it doesn't stifle an ability to listen about another way that may be more relevant for the subject at hand. The more we're willing to listen and accept alternative [perspectives], the more value we create for our shareholders.

Bye has been a leader in the area of fostering and leveraging diversity at Air Products, as have Huck and McAndrew. The Executive Forum for Diversity was formed over a year ago with the mission to drive the kinds of changes the company needs to create a culture that values difference. Bye notes that "As we've looked at this, one of the things that has emerged is the perception that there is a success model at Air Products that includes qualities such as type A, engineering background, logic-driven approach, etc. We'd like to promote appreciating different styles. We'd like to be able to counsel people on how they can add value to the group, not on how they should behave to conform to a certain image. To do that, we need to promote a culture that allows for different types to succeed."

Regarding gender, Bye notes that women seem to be more successful in breaking the glass ceiling in finance than in other areas. In fact, Bye feels that the controllership function is very progressive in diversity and related areas:

As a function, controllership is ahead in a lot of areas, diversity being one of them, but in a number of employee satisfaction areas as well. Controllership tends to score well on surveys of employee satisfaction. They celebrate things, publicize promotions, give team rewards.... There's a lot that other areas can learn from controllership, and I'd like to see controllership be proactive at teaching not only issues relevant to finance but issues in other areas as well. Our controllership is absolutely ahead of the game.

Bye stated that HR has developed intensive leadership training modules that address leverage competencies, including one on diversity. He feels that this training "has helped to really make a difference." The leadership training modules will be discussed below.

Overall, Bye views the controllership function as making great strides in reaching its goal of being a strategic, forward-thinking business partner, and he regards leverage competencies as an important part of that process.

Financial Leadership at Air Products: An HR Perspective

Jay McAndrew views competencies that are important to finance people as largely the same as those for others in the organization. He stressed adaptability—the ability to thrive in an ever more complex, changing, global environment. In addition, he mentioned cooperation as another core competency, and, like Huck and Bye, noted the closer, more strategic ties of finance to business. In this regard, he stated, "Historically, we tended to operate in a silo environment. Those who can get out of their own paradigms and cut across various organizations will do well."

McAndrew went on to cite the competencies mentioned by Huck and Bye. Like Bye, he emphasized interpersonal understanding and leveraging diversity:

> We are working very hard on fostering diversity and on diversity training. Recently, senior people from across the world spent a week on diversity training—understanding diversity, developing a business case for it, communicating it throughout the organization, and then living it. It's a very challenging subject, and it's related to interpersonal understanding.

HR has focused on the generic area of leadership development. McAndrew discusses this in some detail:

> Historically, if you wanted to get ahead in the finance organization, you did it through technical competence.... Our efforts over the years were successful. We have a good, strong finance organization at Air Products. As we grew and changed, however, we realized

there was a gap between what we are and what we should be in providing leadership to the company in finance and other functions. We were always focused on the technical areas. We never said to a senior financial manager, "You're not only responsible for the technical competence of finance, you're also responsible for the morale, leadership, and nurturing of your people." We decided to invest in the development of leaders.

We started a leadership education process four years ago. It focuses on the fundamental responsibilities of a leader. We started by getting people to understand their own personalities. Each participant completed a personality profile and a 360-degree review. Each participant got a lot of value out of that assessment.

We then went on to another module on performance enhancement, which focuses not only on what you're accomplishing but how you're getting there. A third module focused on change management—how to manage change and promote teamwork. The fourth module was devoted to diversity, and the fifth to more advanced leadership strategies. Our finance executives, from our most senior person down through our middle management, have all participated. Modules are three to five days in length.

Figure 4.1 briefly outlines the five leadership education modules. Figure 4.2 lists capabilities/competencies expected of leaders at Air Products.

In addition to the leadership modules, HR offers a wide variety of internal training courses to develop leadership competencies. These include self-directed or professionally led training sessions. Figure 4.3 is a sample of course offerings, taken from an HR training course catalogue. HR also offers employees external training courses. Managers may come to HR informally for advice about what is available to help develop a subordinate who may, for example, have poor interpersonal skills. McAndrew notes that "We have some extremely capable people who had difficulty relating to other people.... We have utilized external courses to supplement our internal offerings. We have also offered executive counseling to senior people. We have numerous opportunities to get people the right help—whether internal or external."

Figure 4.1
Air Products' Leadership Education Curriculum Plan

MODULE ONE: CREATING STRATEGIC ALIGNMENT

An overview of the corporation's expectations of those in leadership roles, defining responsibilities and accountabilities. An opportunity to gain greater understanding of:

- Yourself as a leader at Air Products to increase your effectiveness, and enhance your ability to improve effectiveness of your organization, and

- Our fundamentals. . .Our future and how leaders can insure that our values and vision are woven into the functioning of their organizations.

MODULE TWO: ACHIEVING PEAK PERFORMANCE. . .CREATING LINE OF SIGHT

Will provide Air Products management with a strong foundation in the management and leadership skills critical to success in today's global, performance-driven business world.

MODULE THREE: LEADING THE CHANGE MANAGEMENT PROCESS

An opportunity to examine the leader's role in diagnosing the need for change and implementing change, while increasing our leaders' capacity to manage both the change process and themselves as change agents.

MODULE FOUR: CREATING AND LEADING TEAMS THAT MAXIMIZE DIVERSITY

Focus on developing and leading high performance teams and the leadership actions and skills necessary to: create, value, support and sustain diverse teams, improve team performance, and shape organizational environments to maximize diversity and teamwork.

MODULE FIVE: LEADERSHIP STRATEGIES

A synthesizing (or capstone) experience focusing on topics of primary importance for continued outstanding leadership; e.g., ethics, systems thinking, and measures of leadership.

Figure 4.2
The Air Products Leader

Successful leaders will model these behaviors, demonstrate these capabilities and apply these skills, both within their own sphere of influence and to achieve optimal results for the good of the corporation.

Leaders:

- Understand the Strategic Issues
- Analyze the Issues and Use Sound Judgment
- Successfully Manage Execution
- Optimize Processes and Systems
- Effectively Influence Others
- Achieve Success Through Teams
- Drive for Peak Performance
- Successfully Coach and Develop People
- Relentlessly Champion Change
- Value Diversity
- Foster Open Communication
- Demonstrate Work Commitment
- Accept Personal Responsibility and Accountability
- Demonstrate Adaptability
- Sustain an Environment of Trust
- Use Financial and Quantitative Data to Make Decisions—"Manage by Fact"
- Possess Business Knowledge and Acumen
- Demonstrate a Focus on Customer Needs

HR on Competency Development

Thus, a variety of tools for leadership competency development exist at Air Products. McAndrew notes, however, that for many, developing and applying these skills can be extremely difficult.

If you don't possess the natural ability, trying to acquire the leadership competencies can be challenging, particularly if you've grown up in an environment that didn't reward that kind of behavior. Historically at Air Products, the ladder to success was via functional competence.

Figure 4.3
Human Resources Training Course Catalog

Handling Others' Emotions Under Pressure—Techniques are provided to help you remain calm and objective, recover quickly, and help others do the same. Learn to take charge in emotional situations to keep the discussion moving forward. *Length: 4 hours*

Influence: Collaborating for Results—*Influence=the ability to get work done with people over whom you have no direct control or authority.* Focus on the process and techniques for building, using, and sustaining influence. Confidential feedback on influencing skills is gathered from six selected associates and a summary is provided during class for assessment and planning. *Length: 2-1/2 days*

Leadership Through Teamwork—Prepares leaders to form, develop, and lead teams. Learn to increase team effectiveness, foster collaboration, trust, teamwork, and resolve conflicts within the team. Prework involves a team effectiveness assessment tool to be completed by participant and team members. Confidential summary report is provided to each participant during the class for review and action planning. *Length: 2-1/2 days*

Managing Your Priorities and Your Workload—Learn how to handle competing priorities, coordinate and negotiate responsibilities, schedules, and resources with others, delegate or hand off tasks, and handle interruptions and requests for help effectively. *Length: 4 hours*

Myers-Briggs Type Indicator®: Intro and the MBTI—*For Individual Contributors.* Gain an understanding of the Myers-Briggs Type Indicator® and your own personality type. Learn about the other types and how this information can be applied to become more effective in the workplace. *Length: 4 hours*

Myers-Briggs Type Indicator®: Leadership and the MBTI—*For Managers, Supervisors, Team Leads.* Learn about your personality type and what it has to do with your leadership style, including how you manage change. Learn the effect various personality types have on a work group, team department, and the company. *Length: 7 hours*

Negotiating Across Cultures (International Negotiation Skills)—Addresses the basics of negotiating from both a transactional and relational perspective. Provides a variety of practical analytical and planning tools that can be applied to the complexities of negotiating with representatives of different cultures. Techniques are applied to case studies and actual ongoing negotiations. *Length: 2 days*

Negotiating Win/Win—*For negotiations within the United States.* Build awareness and skills in negotiation planning strategies, phases of a negotiation, distinguishing wants from needs, determining the tangible and intangible resources that can be exchanged, and selecting tactics and countertactics. *Length: 2 days*

On the other hand, McAndrew has seen a number of people grow and develop in their competencies:

I have seen some people who have experienced dramatic change, and it was a function of simply expanding their self-awareness. There are a number of individuals who have come through the leadership education process who take it very seriously and have made noticeable improvement in their leadership abilities.

Regarding competency development within the finance function, McAndrew states, "Frankly, I would say that at Air Products our financial team has taken the program seriously. Our VP and controller is very involved in our diversity effort, as well as in [facilitating] communications on the subject. A lot more time is being spent on people issues."

Like Bye, McAndrew emphasized the place of experience in the development of competencies:

Having diverse experiences outside the functional area is particularly helpful [for competency development]. We've been successful in moving finance people into key commercial areas....We've taken finance people and moved them to HR....There are informal and formal mechanisms to do so. Formally, we have a Human Resources Planning Process.

Each year, our operating and staff units go through a human resources planning process. They identify high potential employees—employees who need to be moved or developed. There are specific plans made for individuals to gain different work experiences. At the corporate level, we have the Management Organization Development Committee (MODC), which reviews middle and senior management positions, succession plans, and developmental moves.

Competencies and Performance Enhancement Reviews

Sometimes, training plans are incorporated into an employee's career development discussion. Specific actions and behaviors to be improved are outlined in development plans. Module Two of leadership education includes training in the performance enhancement process.

For the controllership function, an important part of performance enhancement is the competency ladder. Competencies are grouped into four categories: personal skills, leadership skills, technical skills, and functional skills. Both the employee and the supervisor rank the employee on various behaviorally based dimensions. It is expected that an employee at a certain grade level within the function will demonstrate certain levels of competence.

The joint competency assessments are followed by dialogues between supervisor and employee about where the employee's strengths reside and where there are development needs. A development plan is outlined that is designed to facilitate growth/mastery of various competencies. This plan may include specific job experiences or training to develop competencies, which may be incorporated into performance reviews and career discussions.

A separate competency assessment guide has been developed for more senior management.

Figure 4.4 outlines the categories of controllership competencies. Figure 4.5 is an example of a competency description (teamwork) at different levels of mastery. Figure 4.6 is a template for competency assessments of managers/supervisors.

Summary

Taking the controllership, business, and HR perspectives as a whole, a consistent picture emerges regarding the place of competencies and competency development for finance associates (again, the emphasis was on the controllership function, owing to the C2K initiative). Consistent with the COO's call for a future-oriented focus, they all emphasize the significance of the changing, more strategic, business partner role for finance. Furthermore, they all see the critical role leverage competencies play in facilitating the success of finance people as business partners.

Competency and leadership development at Air Products is a work in progress. Great strides have been made in recent years, facilitated in controllership through structural changes, and supported at the highest levels of the company. The company's senior executives hope

Figure 4.4
Controllership Competencies Skill Groups

Four sets of skill groups have been defined for Controllership professionals. The Personal and Leadership skill groups are common to all areas, while the Functional Knowledge competencies are what truly differentiate each specialty from the others. Listed below are the competency groups and subcategories that address key skills and abilities.

PERSONAL SKILLS
- Interpersonal
- Communication
- Teamwork
- Problem Solving and Creativity

LEADERSHIP SKILLS
- Planning and Organizing
- Leading and Influencing
- Employee Development

TECHNICAL SKILLS
- Computer Skills
- Business/Process Awareness

FUNCTIONAL SKILLS

Credit	Accounting	Audit	Analysis
■ Credit/ Collections (Receivables Management)	■ Accounting Theory and Knowledge ■ Accounting Application	■ Accounting Theory and Knowledge ■ Auditing Knowledge ■ Gathering and Evaluating Information ■ Evaluating Internal Controls ■ Preparing and Reviewing Workpapers and Reports ■ Computer Skills (IS Only)	■ Accounting Theory and Knowledge ■ Financial Analysis Theory ■ Applications of Analysis Skills

Figure 4.5
Skill Competency Level Descriptions

Skill Group: Personal
Skill Category: Teamwork
Ability to cooperate and collaborate with others toward the pursuit of common goals

Competency Level	Competency Description	Examples/Comments
Level 5	■ Encourages a team to work together to accomplish its goals. ■ Is an effective major contributor on larger projects. ■ Supports team outcome regardless of individual impact. ■ Demonstrates initiative by doing prework on ideas before team meetings.	
Level 6	■ Effectively resolves conflict within the team. ■ Reevaluates, communicates, and redirects team priorities. ■ Helps team set realistic and attainable goals.	
Level 7	■ Demonstrates the ability to participate effectively on cross-functional teams both inside and outside the company. ■ Clearly expresses the goals to others in the organization. ■ Builds on thoughts of others.	
Level 8	■ Facilitates group interaction and actively employs the team talents of all participants. ■ Creates an environment in which the contributions of each team member are recognized, encouraged, and supported. ■ Demonstrates the ability to participate effectively with diverse groups of all levels both within and outside the company. ■ Listens and probes others to ensure understanding. ■ Selects, creates, and commissions new teams. ■ Cites team efforts over individual recognition.	
Level 9	■ Expertly establishes and manages multidisciplinary teams. ■ Leads teams in support of higher-level organizational goals. ■ Ensures workload is evenly and appropriately distributed. ■ Fosters honesty and integrity in a nonthreatening environment. ■ Initiates recognition for team accomplishments.	

Figure 4.6
Competency Assessment Guide—Manager/Supervisor

Name_____ Prepared by _____
Current Position _____ Grade _____
Years in Current Position _____ Years with Company_____

Competency	Score	Dimension
	1-7*	
Leadership		■ Personally innovative
Management/Supervisory		■ Open to new ideas
Comments:		■ Communications
		■ Treats others with respect
		■ Inspires
		■ Develops people
		■ Builds and develops teams
		■ Integrity/Trust
Total Leadership		
Business Skills		■ Strategic Focus
Comments:		■ Vision
		■ Risk-taking
		■ Judgment
Total Business Skills		
Functional Skills		■ Accounting
Comments:		■ Operational Analysis
		■ Capital Analysis
Total Functional Skills		

Best Assignment Now:

Ultimate Potential (Grade):
Redeployment or Change in Role: Yes_____   No_____

Type of Position:

Skills Supporting Move:

Is this person in Top 80%?   Yes_____   No_____

USE REVERSE SIDE FOR ADDITIONAL COMMENTS

*Score 1-7 with 7 highest and 4 average

and expect to see even more progress in this area in the future. Fostering and leveraging diversity is especially important.

Figure 4.7 diagrams the processes involved in facilitating the development of leverage competencies for controllership at Air Products. At the center of the diagram is finance as business partner. This highlights the fact that finance's strategic role increases the importance of developing leverage competencies. C2K is placed parenthetically here to emphasize that this initiative has enhanced the strategic place of finance at

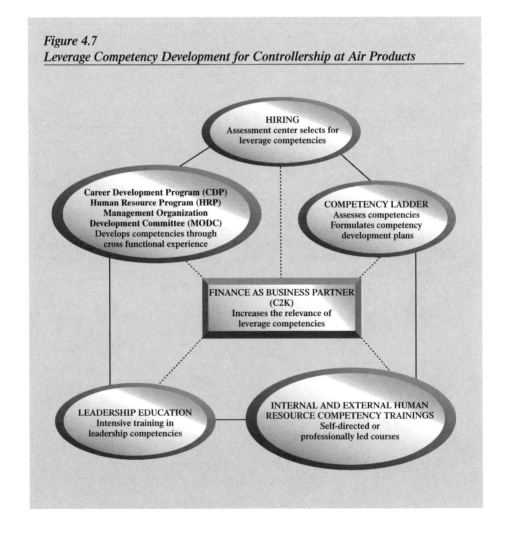

Figure 4.7
Leverage Competency Development for Controllership at Air Products

Air Products. The hiring process selects for many of these competencies among MBA job candidates. CDP, HRP, and MODC facilitate the growth of these competencies through cross-functional experience. Leadership Education provides direct training in leadership competencies, and HR also provides other direct internal and external training for leadership development. The competency ladder directly assesses competencies and provides for competency development plans to be incorporated into the performance enhancement process. The lines connecting the processes serve to emphasize that they interact with and facilitate one another.

Endnote

1. Additional information can be found on the Web at www.airproducts.com.

Bristol-Myers Squibb Company

Company Background

Leadership development is the number one business priority of Bristol-Myers Squibb (B-MS). In a special report, *Our Leadership Team for the Future,*[1] Charles A. Heimbold, Jr., the company's chairman and CEO, states,

> At Bristol-Myers Squibb, we want people who are smart and focused. But we also want people with great values—people who care, people who are passionate about the future and the possibilities of our business, who take nothing for granted and understand that our goals are achievable if we work together. We want people who are highly creative, highly motivated, and highly productive. Simply put, we want leaders. That's why leadership development is at the top of our list of key business objectives. It is, in fact, objective number one.

Charles Heimbold has been chairman since 1994. Since taking the helm, he has put in place a new leadership team—but, more important, he has set in motion a company-wide emphasis on leadership development that will affect every B-MS employee in the years to come.

All senior executives at B-MS participate in extensive leadership development. The chairman's stated mandate is to extend this process throughout the entire company. For a highly decentralized organization of more than 55,000 employees, operating in almost every country around the globe, this is clearly an ambitious goal. However, it is a mandate that must be met, insists Charles G. Tharp, senior vice president, human resources:

We're changing only leaders—not objectives or values or strategies. That's why our corporate priority is to develop leadership at all levels, and not just a handful of top leaders. Leadership is collective—that is, it's not individual leaders that make a difference, but the existence of leadership at all levels of the company. Leadership is all about people who can reach out, act as a team, and share their learnings as they move throughout the organization. In a company of 55,000 people, one person can't really make much happen alone. What he or she can do is energize others, and that's what this is all about.

Leadership development at B-MS cuts equally across all functions and businesses. No job-level distinctions are made about its importance or its applicability. This case study focuses on how these company-wide values and leadership development initiatives are embraced and implemented by the finance professionals. It also describes how B-MS HR professionals are adapting leadership tools to the specific job functions and developmental paths of financial executives.

The Finance Organization at B-MS

Finance at B-MS has always been viewed as a function—but a function that is highly integrated into the businesses. Most of the company's finance people report directly to the heads of business operations on a straight-line basis. They also report, on a dotted-line basis, to the company's senior vice president and chief financial officer, Michael F. Mee, and to the company's vice president, financial operations and controller, Frederick S. Schiff. Only a small, centralized group of about 30 finance professionals is located at corporate headquarters. (Some of CFO Mee's views on leadership are summarized in figure 5.1.)

Of the company's decentralization and the resulting integration of finance professionals into the businesses, Fred Schiff notes,

If I had to put a number on the finance people in our organization, it is probably somewhere between three and four thousand. While our people have finance skills and finance backgrounds, they are really an integral part of our businesses. Finance runs very deep in our organization and all of our employees know they must be able

Figure 5.1
Leadership Development—A View from the CFO

Michael F. Mee is senior vice president and chief financial officer at Bristol-Myers Squibb. Mee is one of the seven direct reports to the chairman. With Global Business Services under his direction, Mee has been charged with taking a 1,500-person organization and driving effectiveness and productivity throughout the B-MS organization. With more than 20 years of experience as a financial executive and as a leader in his own right, Mee, during our interviews at B-MS, shared some telling observations about leadership and the leadership development process.

- The people who are most adaptable probably have the best shot at being leaders.

- At the end of the day we are looking for highly motivated people. People who know what they have to do—and get it done.

- Leadership skills boil down to something I learned a long time ago—organizations, in most cases, value individuals for their variety of experiences, as opposed to someone who I would label as "Ivory Soap proficient" (i.e., an individual who is 99.99 percent knowledgeable but only about one thing).

- Vision is important, but it usually comes from experience and learning how to work with the ideas and the people around you.

- There are many first-rate leaders across corporate America today, but when I think of them, vision would not be the first thing that came to mind. Certainly, they are resourceful, insightful, tough-minded, committed, love their work, love what they are doing—but they are not necessarily all visionaries.

- Leadership is about knowing the endgame—here's what I am up against, here's who I am up against—it's less about vision than getting down to tough work.

- There are many interesting people out there with interesting ideas—but most don't work. When it comes to leadership, we are looking for results. I cannot emphasize a results orientation enough!

- By way of a special genetic code, I am not sure finance people bring anything unique to the leadership table. But they can be objective about things, and numbers are the common denominator across all businesses. By working with manufacturing, marketing, and research they have a real opportunity that others don't have to gain broad experiences that might work elsewhere. From an experiential point of view, finance people have a real leadership development advantage.

to talk the numbers. Finance people are very fortunate in that everyone understands what it means to meet or not meet your budget. Accordingly, they are welcome participants at the business decision-making tables of our organization. If you asked our marketing people about finance, if anything they would say they want even more finance people involved in their businesses.

Even with this decentralization, however, from a leadership perspective there is still a distinct finance organization at B-MS. No matter where they are located, finance professionals have clear and coordinated development paths. These paths are facilitated by the culture of the finance organization, which places significant importance on internal communication. A concerted effort is made to know every person in the finance organization and to identify the development opportunities for which they are best suited.

Identifying Finance Leaders—The Saddlebrook Group

According to Heimbold,

> To be a successful leader in our organization, you must be continuously creating other leaders. You exert enormous influence on an organization through the people you develop and put into leadership positions.

The finance leaders at B-MS embrace this quote, which encompasses the foundation and mission for the entire company's leadership development process. Moreover, it gives the top financial leaders at the company the mandate to develop future financial leaders. And it places upon their shoulders the direct responsibility to do so throughout the entire finance organization.

The Saddlebrook Group is a good illustration of how this leadership development responsibility is implemented. A few years ago, Schiff asked the top finance executives at the company—approximately 15, including senior financial executives from both corporate headquarters and the worldwide businesses—to meet regularly on technical financial issues affecting the company. The group is now known as the Saddlebrook Group.

It was not long, however, before these meetings—now held more than four times a year—began to shift their emphasis from technical matters to the very leadership responsibilities articulated by Heimbold: namely, to create new leaders. Schiff elaborates:

Today, 75 percent of these meetings are spent on leadership development. We talk about the financial executive leadership positions that are available throughout B-MS and who we think might best fill each position. Our focus is on development, on who is best for each job in terms of fulfilling the experiences needed in order to move on to the next level of leadership responsibility. We are always thinking one or two positions ahead.

Members of the Saddlebrook Group travel quite extensively. They spend a great deal of time meeting and getting to know the financial talent in the organization. Therefore, even though finance is highly integrated into the individual businesses, everyone is working together to identify the best talent at B-MS and, even more important, getting to know that talent personally. The culture of the finance organization is based on communication.

Developing Finance Leaders—Experiential Learning

When it comes to developing leaders at the company, Tharp gets to the heart of the matter:

We believe that experience is the greatest teacher, so moving people into new roles, with new opportunities for learning, is the best way to aid in their business development.

Experiential learning is fundamental to the leadership development process of all B-MS financial executives. This is evident from the time a finance person enters the company to the time that person would be identified as an up-and-coming financial executive warranting the attention of the Saddlebrook Group.

The company has an entry-level MBA program, called the Financial Associates Program, headed by Schiff. Each year the company recruits five to ten financial associates. These individuals come from business schools such as Columbia, Duke, Cornell, and Darden. Since the program began it has had a very high retention rate, which today is excellent for MBAs. The program aims to attract individuals who are considering finance but are also interested in a rotation program that provides varied initial business experiences. The program is successful because it rotates these individuals throughout B-MS, permitting them to experience the company's businesses and meet people. After 18 to 24 months, these individuals are expected to locate a position within the company.

The Financial Associates Program is a bridge to the culture of the company. While the company does not have a "promote only from within" policy, many high-level finance people began their career through the program. The program's rotational emphasis also establishes real work experiences. Finance people at B-MS transfer throughout the organization more than any other workers in the company—on average, they take a new position every two years.

Summing up, Schiff states,

> The MBAs we hire have the financial skill set. That's not even an issue. The real issue is how they work with the management team and the marketing, planning, and production people of our company. There is no financial skill-training here for MBAs. That's why they went to the best business schools in the country. It is an experiential training program, and that's the way we always have treated it. As long as I have been here, the successful finance associates are not those who prove themselves to be technically more competent than others. Instead, they are the individuals who demonstrate they understand the businesses of B-MS and the relevant underlying strategic issues and have the ability to convey those issues effectively to others within the organization.

Experiential development does not end with the Finance Associates Program. On the contrary, it is really only the beginning, and a direct reflection of what financial professionals can expect as they move forward on their career paths in the organization.

Schiff observes,

> We are very bottom-line oriented around here. Generally, the more experiences finance people successfully complete, the more they are in demand by the rest of the organization. We will work with every finance person in trying to get them the experiences they need to move forward in the organization. In the end, however, everyone has an opportunity to create their own demand based

upon whether others see them as adding value to the organization or not.

Echoing Schiff's observation, Sandra Holleran, vice president, human resources, states,

> We expect our leaders to have knowledge and experience in their functional area. Many individuals are great at developing functional expertise, but some tend to fall short when it comes to developing leadership skills and abilities. What's important is that every individual in the organization takes ownership of their personal development. Moreover, we emphasize that this does not always translate into getting promoted. Instead, at B-MS it means making sure you get the experiences you need to develop yourself as a leader. Many individuals don't think about development in terms of experiences. In today's world, when it comes to developing leaders and leadership skills, it is just as important to be thinking about moving across an organization—experientially—as it is about moving up.

Developing Finance Leaders—Online Position Profiles

At B-MS a clear appreciation of what it takes to be a successful financial leader is reinforced by the company's position profiles. These profiles are available online to everyone. The profiles have been developed for all positions and grade levels. Each profile is broken down into the following developmental categories: expected areas of competence (skills and abilities), leadership behaviors, experience desired, knowledge desired, and developmental value.

In terms of leadership development, these profiles are critical tools because they:

- establish clear standards of performance for positions;

- articulate the leadership behaviors required of all B-MS employees;

- indicate the key experiences and knowledge required for positions; and

- define learning opportunities provided by a specific job position.

Figure 5.2 offers the position profile for financial executives who belong—or aspire—to the Saddlebrook Group. A review of this profile immediately confirms that the skills and abilities required at the executive level of finance are not those of crunching numbers, financial reporting, or controlling the activities of others. Rather, they include the very competencies frequently labeled the soft stuff—communication, self-confidence, and decisiveness—the interpersonal and intrapersonal skills. Moreover, finance professionals at the executive level are also expected to demonstrate certain abilities, such as the ability to translate strategy into operational goals and objectives and to select and develop individuals with the talent to achieve competitive superiority for the company.

In addition to noting these competencies, the position profile in figure 5.2 has powerful prescriptive value for those aspiring to the Saddlebrook Group, offering a clear indication of the experiences and knowledge required. In fact, these very experiences become the main focus as the Saddlebrook members try to identify and develop the future financial leaders of the company. Schiff comments, "When we talk about people at our Saddlebrook meetings we go down the list of competencies, behaviors, and experiences in the executive profile and try to identify and match up the best people. The position profile is the tool we use to decide who is best for what job, or who needs what experience in order to move forward in the organization."

Comparing the position profiles of the company's CFO and finance director in figure 5.2 makes it clear that as individuals move to higher levels of responsibility in the finance organization, the expected areas of competency skills and abilities get broader. The profiles at that level begin to emphasize the importance of interpersonal and intrapersonal competencies.

While the leadership behaviors of a finance director and member of the Saddlebrook Group are very similar, the list of expected competencies for a finance director is far more limited. It focuses more on traditional skills and abilities, such as planning, adaptability, judgment, and monitoring. For a member of the Saddlebrook Group the competencies become broader, including such abilities as leading change, translating strategy into operating objectives, and actively promoting diverse perspectives throughout the entire organization.

Figure 5.2
Position Profile

Position: Finance
Division/Department: Bristol-Myers Squibb (Saddlebrook Group)
Function: Finance/Executive

Expected Areas of Competence (i.e., skills and abilities)

- Creates a compelling vision for the business/function and communicates that vision effectively throughout the organization and to external stakeholders (i.e., customers, the business/professional community, peers and employees at all levels in the organization). Acts as a spokesperson for their business/function.

- Communicates effectively as an official spokesperson for Finance in a variety of settings. Delivers clear and articulate presentations that include defending position on controversial topics, adapting style to audience when planning presentation and communicating succinctly in one-on-one situations.

- Actively promotes using diverse perspectives throughout the entire organization to meet organizational challenges and goals. Advocates that valuing diversity is key for optimal performance.

- Sees novel relationships and thinks ahead in non-incremental ways to develop superior competitive strategies to support growth and productivity priorities.

- Translates strategy into operational goals and objectives, identifies necessary resources (people and capital) and leads the organization to focus on high priority opportunities. Assures their organization follows through to achieve superior execution of plans.

- Selects and develops individuals with the talent necessary to achieve competitive superiority. Guides the leadership development process, ensuring ongoing succession for key positions.

- Creates a high performance, externally focused operating culture throughout the organization which emphasizes the customer, teamwork, personal accountability and winning attitude. Models the desired behaviors personally and reinforces desired behaviors at all levels of the organization.

- Leads change in the organization to continuously adapt to a dynamic business environment. Learns from experience. Reflects on experiences, integrates, and applies learnings to enhance organizational performance.

- Demonstrates self confidence, decisiveness, and risk taking but is not impulsive; has the presence to manage through a crisis.

- Develops strong working relationships with key stakeholders both within and outside the company (i.e., customers, the business/professional community, peers and employees at all levels in the organization).

Figure 5.2
Position Profile (Continued)

Leadership Behaviors

- Delivers results, drives for continuous improvement. Sets high performance expectations and holds others accountable for the results expected. Acts with a sense of urgency.

- Understands needs and considers external customers and/or internal clients in decisions and actions.

- Encourages and supports collaboration across departments and takes actions that are best for B-MS versus individual unit. Is able to work with a wide variety of people.

- Creates new ideas and processes, and encourages others to try new approaches and takes risks. Strives to enhance performance by doing things that are unique and leading edge.

- Willingly embraces changes needed to adapt to new circumstances.

- Provides frequent feedback and coaching to others on ways to improve performance. Is proactive in providing developmental opportunities for others.

- Appropriately shares own viewpoint and opinions, even when they may be negative or unpopular. Encourages the free exchange of information and opinion.

- Willing to ask for support from others, proactively asks how they can support others.

- Genuinely respects other points of view and opinions and demonstrates sensitivity to cultural differences. Seeks out other perspectives and capitalizes on diversity when developing strategies and approaches.

- Willingly owns results, focuses energy on what more they can personally do versus blaming others, finding excuses or being the victim.

- Knows the contributions others are making and acknowledges them. Gives credit to specific individuals or teams.

- Has a winning attitude and instills a passion for winning. An attitude which is demonstrated by a "can do" approach to issues, resilience, commitment to goals, and persistence.

- Demonstrates principled leadership and sound business ethics; shows consistency among principles, values, and behaviors.

- Seeks and welcomes feedback, responds to coaching. Takes action to enhance performance based on experiences and feedback.

- Creates an environment which enhances trust, learning, and risk taking.

Figure 5.2
Position Profile (Continued)

Experiences Desired

- Development of successful strategy and program/product/process implementation.

- Demonstrated ability to get results in complex, possibly adverse conditions.

- Demonstrated track record of selecting talented people, developing them, and exporting them to key roles in the organization.

- Cultural sensitivity gained through international/global responsibility.

- Demonstrated ability to build a team and develop a high performance organization.

- Demonstrated ability to differentially allocate financial resources to achieve superior business performance.

Knowledge Desired

- Mastery of profession and in-depth knowledge of an industry. Able to anticipate industry trends and emerging issues.

- Appreciation of the complexities of cross-functional management issues.

- Knowledge of competitors in the industry and effective competitive strategy.

- Understanding of financial principles and how to leverage this knowledge to make sound business decisions.

- Awareness of social, regulatory and economic issues that may affect the business.

Developmental Value

- Gain increased understanding of B-MS strategy and key drivers required to successfully grow the business.

- Enhance ability to manage complex systems.

- Development of the sensitivity and skill to address issues involving multiple internal and external stakeholders.

- Increased demand to balance multiple, possibly competing priorities.

- Opportunity to lead large scale organization change.

Building an Integrated Perspective—
The Leadership Model

It is important to reiterate that developing the depth, breadth, and diversity of global leadership talent is the company's number-one growth priority. All leaders at B-MS are responsible for developing leadership in the organization.

The B-MS leadership model is illustrated in figure 5.3. The leadership messages that the model outlines are clear. At B-MS, leaders must demonstrate or seek to develop in others the following:

- Functional expertise—largely the professional responsibility of the individual;

- Leadership behaviors—as contained in the position profiles and the focus of much of the personal developmental support provided at B-MS (see below); and

- Capacity—a new element of the leadership model that incorporates the knowledge and experiences that one brings to the company.

Figure 5.3
Leadership Model

Expectations of Leaders at Bristol-Myers Squibb

- Create and articulate a vision
- Set priorities and allocate resources
- Drive innovation by embracing diversity and change
- Take accountability and achieve results
- Set the example and thereby shape the culture
- Develop self and develop others

A Leader Needs the Following:

- **Functional expertise**—includes knowledge and experience in a certain functional area
- **Capacity is the cornerstone**—This is what you, as an individual, bring to the organization
- **Leadership behaviors**—Those behaviors that represent a high performance culture

As an educational tool, the model seeks to fully reflect all aspects of leadership development. It also reveals leadership development as a work in progress; recent additions include cognitive and emotional capacities. By emphasizing the model in conjunction with the position profiles, the company has established a "best practices" leadership standard for all positions—including finance.

Holleran elaborates on this important relationship:

> The leadership model and the position profiles clarify expectations, help in creating a development plan, specify the learning value of a role, define standards for selection into a position, and help employees gain a good understanding of the B-MS culture. For a developmental dialogue to take place it must start with some standards: namely, an awareness of expectations that will help anchor one's career dialogue discussions and allow one to set realistic goals. That's the importance of understanding the leadership model and its relationship to each individual's position profile.

Combining the leadership model and the position profiles is the basis of building a development case for an individual. The Saddlebrook Group may use both to decide what developmental experiences an individual needs before moving on in the organization.

The Center for Leadership Development

Speaking about the implications of the B-MS leadership model, Holleran explains,

> One's development at the company is largely a shared responsibility. Employees are personally responsible for their own performance, and the employee and manager are jointly accountable for performance enhancement, which includes the following: (1) the employee seeking and welcoming feedback on performance and (2) the manager providing frequent feedback, coaching, and development opportunities. Knowledge and experience in a functional area, such as finance, is expected from our finance leaders as well as leadership behaviors that support a high-performance culture. We spend a lot of time with our employees helping them understand the expectations of leaders at B-MS.

To fulfill this promise, B-MS has established a substantial in-house inventory of leadership development tools and programs. The company also demonstrated its commitment to the leadership development process by creating the Center for Leadership Development (CLD) in 1996. The mission of the CLD is to "assure the development, renewal and continuity of the leadership and operating culture needed to create and sustain competitive superiority in a dynamic global business environment." Currently, the CLD focuses mainly on supporting the company's number one growth priority: "developing the depth, breadth, and diversity of global leadership talent at every level by creating broad, global, and enterprise-wide initiatives that support this objective."[2]

B-MS also recently established the Leadership Development Institute, which emphasizes the importance of "leaders teaching leaders." Its charter is to provide programs focusing on leadership development at every level. What is interesting about the Institute is that line managers, drawn from middle and senior management ranks around the globe, facilitate all programs (forums). Some of the special forums now offered by the Institute include Leading Innovation, Leading Change, Profile of a Leader, Learning to Lead, Building a Pipeline of Talent, and Leaders at Every Level.[3] Note that the Leadership Development Institute has no special courses for finance people, nor are any functional courses in finance offered. Everyone in the company proceeds through the same leadership development training. Also, program participation is always cross-functional, reflecting the company's business and cultural environment.

Figure 5.4 highlights some of the Performance Partnership[4] tools currently used throughout B-MS. Again, none of these leadership development tools are for finance people only. They are used to help develop leaders across all functions and businesses of the B-MS organization.

Figure 5.4
Performance Partnerships

Since development at B-MS is largely a personal responsibility, then how does one go about implementing this most important responsibility? What mechanisms are in place to ensure success? Moreover, what are the responsibilities of the organization and its managers to support the leadership development process of everyone in the organization? In short, what keeps the leadership development process at B-MS in the forefront of everyone's thoughts and moving forward on a day-to-day basis?

To answer these questions, it is important to note that all leadership development at B-MS takes place in the context of a well-structured framework called "Performance Partnerships." These partnerships—as well as the leadership model—apply to everyone at B-MS. Accordingly, it is important to note the essential components of the program as they directly affect the process of how finance leaders are brought along in the organization.

The Career Dialogue is critical to the success of Performance Partnerships. An extension of Performance Partnerships, it is designed to facilitate and enhance continued development by helping employees identify and communicate their career goals.

The elements of the Career Dialogue are as follows:

- Know your career aspirations—including work/life balance considerations.

- Communicate these aspirations to your manager—as part of the ongoing Performance Partnership discussions.

- Learn and understand what the standards of performance are, for your current job and any potential future job—as embodied in the online position profiles available for all job positions and grade levels.

- Seek feedback and coaching to identify experiences that will help you develop and work toward fulfilling your career aspirations.

To help prepare for the career dialogue, all employees are encouraged to complete a "Career Dialogue Summary." This summary helps employees think about their career aspirations, which include acquiring new knowledge, skills, and abilities to improve performance in one's current job. These career dialogues are conducted with an individual's manager as part of one's ongoing Performance Partnership discussions. An individual's manager is considered to be the primary partner in the dialogue. HR generalists are available to provide additional support, if needed.

Leadership Development at B-MS— A Continuing Work in Progress

From the array of leadership development mechanisms, one might conclude that leadership development at B-MS is near completion, which is certainly not the case. Leadership development at B-MS is viewed very much as a work in progress. For example, the leadership model and position profiles have always emphasized the importance of functional skill development, demonstrated behaviors, and certain interpersonal/intrapersonal competencies. However, not until recently have cognitive and emotional capacities become a highlighted component of the leadership development model and process.

Additions and new perspectives on leadership development create new challenges and opportunities. As Holleran concludes, "We have just introduced to our leadership model 'capacity'; namely, the experience and knowledge one brings to the organization. Clearly, for the leadership model to be complete, one must address the area of cognitive capacity. The real and continuing challenge we face at B-MS is how do you integrate functional expertise, capacity, and leadership to create a high-performance leadership team?"

Summary

Financial executive leadership development at B-MS is woven into the culture and fabric of the organization. The leadership model, together with the position profiles, form an important foundation for

- clarifying expectations;

- providing a basis for ongoing career dialogues;

- helping to create a development plan for an individual;

- specifying the experiential value of a specific role;

- defining the standards for selection into a position; and

- helping individuals better understand the culture of B-MS.

The development of all leaders at B-MS emphasizes the importance of integrating functional, behavioral, emotional, and cognitive competencies, as demonstrated by numerous activities and processes. Some of the most notable ones include the role of the Saddlebrook Group in identifying future financial leaders; the significance of varied learning experiences as part of the development process; and the role of position profiles and the leadership model.

Endnotes

1. The report, published in December 1998, continues to set the tone for leadership development at B-MS. The quotes by Chairman Heimbold and Dr. Charles G. Tharp cited throughout this chapter have been excerpted from this report.

2. Quotes are from the B-MS special internal Web site dedicated to leadership development. Some of the links include What is expected of leaders at B-MS? How do I develop my career? How do I develop others?–A Manager's Guide; and How do I develop others?–An Employee Guide.

3. All these forums are focused on the important growth theme of "leaders teaching leaders." For example, the forum Learning to Lead includes a 3.5-day train-the-trainer session to prepare facilitators to teach the course—including a session called Teaching Leaders to Teach.

4. Performance Partnerships at B-MS facilitate leadership development through ongoing feedback and coaching. Career Dialogues—discussed in figure 5.4—are a tool for the extension of the Performance Partnership process.

6

Dana Corporation

The Leadership Challenges

D ana's past chairman, Southwood (Woody) Morcott, first defined his company's global ambitions in 1990. The plan was named Dana 2000, and according to the company, was one of the first programs of its kind to focus on the global business and leadership challenges of the new millennium.

Under Dana 2000, the company redefined its core businesses and realigned its operations worldwide to reflect its global business priorities. Dana 2000 resulted in eight core operations, or strategic business units (SBUs), located in four geographic regions: Europe, North America, Latin America, and Asia. It would be in these SBUs and geographic locations that Dana would meet its competition head-on by producing and distributing its automotive products on a global basis.

Chairman Morcott's vision was to ensure that 90 percent of Dana's business would be in these core product areas. He also specified that Dana's 1990 revenues of approximately $5 billion would have to double by the year 2000, and that for Dana to be recognized as a global player, at least 50 percent of these revenues would have to be derived from international operations. Dana's international sales were only 26 percent of total revenues in 1990.

In response to these formidable leadership challenges, Morcott pushed ahead to transform Dana into a truly global organization. At the end of 1998, Dana's sales stood at $12.5 billion. The top three American automotive producers are clients, and today 28 of the world's 30 largest automotive producers are major customers of Dana. The company's automotive components and systems are used in more than 95 percent of the world's 700 million motor vehicles.

Dana's emphasis on being global—but local in presence—has led to some dramatic leadership challenges and implications for the company. Dana has cut its corporate staff in Toledo, Ohio, to just about 100 people. According to former Executive Vice President and CFO John (Jack) S. Simpson,[1] "Dana is not a complex company to understand, but in a relatively short time period we have become more global than General Motors or Chrysler. Today, the company is located in 32 countries with our war rooms—330 major facilities." This front-line advance of Dana's troops applies equally to finance. Today, more than two-thirds of the company's 600 finance professionals are located in plants outside the United States.

However, Dana still faces considerable challenges as it moves forward with its global ambitions. For example, in 1988 the company was an organization of some 50,000 people. Today, through recent acquisitions, the company's employee population has jumped to over 80,000. As Simpson notes, "Today, almost half of our employees have been with us for less than two years. How do we inculcate them effectively with the Dana way of doing things—the financial systems, the financial controls, and the leadership psyche? It is a real challenge equally impacting all disciplines in this company."

Easing these strains, and facilitating a coordinated spirit of cooperation, is the Dana culture, embodied in what is called the Dana Style. With the company's emphasis on experiential learning, promoting from within, and a clear vision and plan for leadership succession, Dana has positioned itself to meet the leadership challenges of the new millennium. All these elements of the Dana approach to leadership development are discussed in the following sections.

The Dana Style

What is the Dana Style and why is it so important to both the success of the organization and the leadership aspirations of its employees?

Although there are many elements to the Dana Style, overall it is quite straightforward and simple. In many ways it can be summed up as an uncompromising commitment to participation and involvement. As Simpson states, "The Dana Style is a culture that goes back to the founders of this company. It is now the responsibility of Mr. Joseph

Magliochetti, the current chairman to inculcate that style and pass it on to the next generation of leaders at our company."

Even an outside observer comes away with the feeling that Dana employees are active participants in the ongoing activities of the organization. Here are a few notable examples of the Dana Style in practice:

1. From the chairman to the CFO to a machine operator, every employee in the company is expected to improve the organization. Accordingly, some people carry with them idea cards. The point of the ideas program is simple—Dana wants your ideas! In fact, the Dana Style expects "two ideas, per person, per month with 80 percent implementation." The Dana Style seeks to make every employee feel that the company wants his or her ideas and that these ideas could be important solutions to the company's problems or improving its businesses. The Dana Style is about drawing people out and making them feel that they are part of an extended family facing common problems. This is evidenced by the fact that, according to the Dana Style, the most important four words any leader can ever speak to a fellow employee are "What do *you* think?"

2. Facilitating this emphasis on total participation and involvement is the Dana Style of promoting *only* from within the organization. As discussed below, employees at Dana know each other very well and spend many years working together in various parts of the organization. For example, during his more than 26 years with Dana, Simpson moved 11 times for the organization, taking on both plant and international assignments. The company has a very low employee turnover rate, and seldom calls on outside consultants and management gurus to help solve Dana's business problems.

3. Dana's approach to educational development also illustrates the emphasis on total participation. Very much in line with avoiding the "not invented here" syndrome is Dana's strong commitment to the ongoing education of its employees—right up to the chairman of the board. At Dana, every employee is required to complete 40 hours of training per year. To help facilitate this practice, the company has established Dana

University, an on-site state-of-the-art educational facility with its own dedicated in-house training staff. Dana University currently has six full-time trainers, all of whom come from Dana's plants. Duncan James, manager of education, who teaches two of the core finance programs required for management certification, is a former Dana plant controller.

The Dana Style is outlined in figure 6.1. Many of its elements are discussed and incorporated directly or indirectly throughout this case study. The elements of the Dana Style form the basis of Dana's approach to leadership development and cannot be separated from it. Dana does not explicitly focus on competencies or specific behaviors of leadership, nor does it need to. These competencies and behaviors have been incorporated into the Dana Style for generations and are deeply rooted in the company's culture. As Simpson observes, "The Dana Style is a long-lasting tradition and we have tried to weave it throughout the organization."

Finally, Simpson continues, the number-one purpose of the Dana Style is to "earn money for our shareholders and increase the value of their investment every year." As Larry Lottier, dean of Dana University, points out, "The Dana Style is a part of a manager's 'soft skills' but that does not mean it is soft and fuzzy. It is really hard business practices. It is people oriented and very much a business discipline."

"The three schools of Dana University are more important today than ever before. Given our growth and expansion pressures, the university gives us a platform to spread the Dana Style of Management both through our core business and technical courses and through students meeting and working with people from other Dana disciplines. I think one of the great benefits one gets when attending Dana University is that exchange of real time experiences working and learning with other Dana people which, I feel, can be as valuable as the course content itself." In fact, Simpson calls the Dana Style the company's "secret competitive business weapon."

Figure 6.1
The Dana Style

PURPOSE
- Earn money for our shareholders and increase the value of their investment every year.

GROWTH
- Improve market share by growing faster than our markets
- #1 or #2 globally
- 6.5% internal growth, 3.5% acquisitions—10% total

PEOPLE
- People are our most important asset
- Finding a better way
- Business is 90% people—10% money
- Educate—40 hours per person per year
- Productive
- Annual performance appraisal
- Encourage diversity
- Identify with Dana
- Dana University
- Two ideas per person per month—80% implemented
- Cross fertilization—cross training—across regions—across business units
- Commitment
- Dana Certified Supervisor
- Encourage all Dana people to be shareholders
- Dana people set their own goals and judge their performance—manage by objectives
- Healthy and safe
- Experts—25 square feet/3 square meters
- Dana people take ownership of their actions
- Pride in Dana people

LEADERSHIP
- Vision of the future
- Ability to change
- Sense of urgency
- Productivity improves every year
- Promote from within based on performance
- Teamwork
- Lead by example
- 4 Magic Words—"What do *you* think?"
- Trust

Figure 6.1
The Dana Style (Continued)

LEADERSHIP (Continued)
- Respect for people—recognition
- Support the growth of people
- Freedom to fail
- Recognize and reward success
- High integrity and ethical standards
- Listen
- Do what's best for all of Dana

PLANNING
- Beyond 2000
- Global Business Unit and Product Strategies
- Regional Strategic Plans
- Hell Week
- Mid-Years

TECHNOLOGY
- World Class

SUPPLIERS
- Expect total quality and value from suppliers
- Recognize important role suppliers play in Dana achieving strategic objectives
- Seek continuous improvement in supplier abilities

ORGANIZATION
- Decentralize
- Five layers of management to World Operating Committee
- Create task forces rather than permanent staff
- Minimize company-wide procedures
- Responsibility with authority
- Entrepreneurship
- Keep facilities under 500 people
- Open door policy

QUALITY
- Continuous improvement
- Measure, Measure, Measure
- Total quality
- Dana Quality Leadership Process with Six Sigma objective
- Benchmark
- Eliminate waste and paper

Figure 6.1
The Dana Style (Continued)

CUSTOMERS
- Total customer satisfaction—passion for service
- Exceed customers' expectations
- Create value for our customers
- Customer focused

COMMUNICATION
- Communicate! Communicate! Communicate!
- Let Dana people know first
- Communication by word of mouth
- Global Communications Meeting

CITIZENSHIP
- Dana will be a good citizen worldwide
- Respect the environment

Experiential Development

Dana does not hire leaders. The company's primary policy, derived from the Dana Style, is to always promote employees (based on performance) from within the organization. Accordingly, experience is the number one training ground for leadership development and advancement at Dana. With the company's global emphasis, international experience ranks at the top of the list. Specifically, to ascend to one of the firm's top 30 executive positions, international experience is a must. Reinforcing this requirement is the company's policy that proficiency in a second language is required for any manager who will be sent to a non-English-speaking country for two years or more. For those slated for a foreign assignment, the company's tuition reimbursement plan covers the cost of foreign language studies. (Simpson speaks both Korean and Mandarin Chinese.)

In addition, any Dana employee aspiring to the upper ranks of management must gain experience in three specialty areas such as finance, marketing, and manufacturing. To facilitate this experiential process, each year Dana transfers managers from its corporate offices to international plant assignments and in return sends managers from its international operations to headquarters assignments. Also reflective of the company's culture is its unique organizational structure that limits management levels to just five—from the factory floor level right up to regional president—once again ensuring a deeper knowledge of the company's businesses.[2]

Simpson explains,

> It is a multiplicity of influences that help build leadership. No doubt, it is character, foresight, and vision. But it is also the hard stuff—the ability to implement capital productivity programs that we are so very keen about here at Dana. Fundamentally, on the leadership side of things, you can talk about whether leadership is an innate quality or one that can be developed over time throughout the experiences of a lifetime. Here at Dana we believe you can take someone from farmland Indiana and plunk them down in Hong Kong or that you can take someone from Africa and plunk them down in New York. Sure it may be a culture shock. But if that individual has the basic skills, the intellect, the character, the personality, and the potential leadership skills, then you must next put some scabs on their head. What do we mean by this? Well, we are not just going to Shanghai or Beijing to conduct business; we are going to Tianjin or Shanyang also. We are not here to have fun, and spend a lot of money being expatriates, and to live a life of luxury and glory. We are here to make money for our shareholders and this is how we are going to do it. The bottom line is that leadership is about learning from experience.

This emphasis on experience clearly pays off for financial executives and the reputation that finance has achieved within the Dana organization. Lottier observes, "I never ran a plant, but early in my career someone told me that if you ever get a plant job the first critical thing you must do is get a controller you have confidence in. One of the strengths we have here at Dana is having financial people with many years of experience focused on understanding the operations and businesses of this company."

Internal Audit: Growing Leaders

Internal audit is where a financial person begins his or her career at Dana. As such, internal audit plays a critical role in determining the type of finance people that join the company. Internal audit has been around for more than 40 years and is clearly the training ground, or boot camp, for individuals aspiring to a financial career at the organization, although many individuals from the internal audit staff later move on to positions of plant, regional, and SBU presidents.

As Melvin H. Rothlisberger, vice president, corporate audit, notes,

> We promote within the company, and audit is one of the few areas at Dana where we are actively recruiting at college campuses. We look at recruiting as a year-round job. Normally what we are looking for is someone with a degree in accounting or finance. We don't have a lot of financial analyst jobs at Dana, so our basic criterion is accounting or a finance degree, with 12 hours in accounting, plus a 3.3 grade average in their major and a 3.0 overall grade point average. We are not looking for stars. We are looking for team players.

Highlighting the experiential theme, Rothlisberger, who heads up the internal audit staff, outlines the developmental process:

1. When they first join the audit staff, we initially place these young people in a plant setting. They need to see what Dana is all about for a couple of years. Dana is a manufacturer, and while the corporate office is a great place to work, it is not where our company makes its money. We want to get these young people to the front lines of our businesses, and as soon as possible. So, in a relatively short time frame, these individuals have a good idea of what a Dana business does and how our accounting system works. They can close the books and do the basics. And this is all accomplished by the time they are finished with their first assignment, approximately 18 to 24 months after first joining the company.

2. We then bring these seasoned individuals to the home-office audit staff—ideally for two years—and give them a broader perspective of the company. While on audit assignment they

get a chance to travel a great deal and see more of the products and plant operations. Most important, while they quickly recognize that everybody is a Dana person, they also see that each plant has its own personality. Just as important, they get to meet a great number of people and experience different management styles. While on audit assignment, they really get involved in the internal audit function. Internal audit is not about giving someone a list of payables and making sure they can add them up correctly or not. Instead it is giving individuals real experience with process auditing. For example, understanding who writes the purchase requisitions, receives the materials, and reconciles the accounts. It is learning about where value is being created or destroyed by various business processes at the company and making suggestions on how to improve things. So by the time they complete their audit assignment, these individuals are ready for their first controller's spot. They have a pretty good idea of what they want to accomplish, and how they must behave and manage others to make it happen.

3. The next step on the development path is the individual's first plant controller's job. Not a big plant—perhaps $20 to $50 million in annual sales, with somewhere between 300 to 500 employees. This may not seem like a large responsibility for a $13 billion company; however, keep in mind, at this time in their careers these individuals are only about 25 or 26 years old. Accordingly, one of the greatest challenges they face is that while they head up the department, they are also likely to be the youngest person in the group. Years ago people at Dana had military experience and the respect for rank. But I am not so sure you see that anymore today. As young plant controllers, perhaps the most important lesson they learn is that while you would like to get a consensus, you simply can't talk about business issues forever. You need to make a decision and get things done.

The internal audit development path outlined above certainly confirms Simpson's comments about the need to give these individuals some real-world experience. In just five or six years, they are ready to move on to larger responsibilities. Once they are at the plant controller level, they have to make a decision about where they want to go next in the organization. For example, do they want to stay in accounting or move on to general management? If they want to stay in finance, they can try to move to a controller assignment at a larger plant.

Here Rothlisberger observes,

> If you now move up to a $250 million plant controller job you now must have the ten people under you doing their best, because you can't do it all by yourself anymore. That's probably the next biggest challenge our young controllers face. Here's where the people and softer skills clearly come into play. One of the things that supports these people is the Dana University training, whereby most of our controllers, at this point, are fully certified as managers. Also, the audit staff has built a common bond and we are fairly comfortable with the informal process of change. Our corporate culture—the Dana Style—has emphasized people and promoting them from within. Change is expected and the related experience highly valued. This company rewards people with opportunity as they grow.

Succession Planning

A clear outgrowth of the company's emphasis on experiential learning and promoting from within is Dana's obsession with leadership succession planning. As Simpson notes, "One thing that we cherish at Dana—it's almost sacrosanct—is our leadership succession program."

The program is straightforward and does not rely on any advanced computer analysis or behavioral assessment tools. It has been around since the company's inception. The key elements of the program are as follows:

1. It currently includes the top 139 jobs in the company—what the company calls its Global Leadership Group.

2. For each of these 139 jobs there is a waiting list of three individuals. The waiting list has fewer than 417 names because some individuals might be designated as possible candidates for more than one job.

3. The selection process is taken very seriously. The company's policy committee goes off site each year for two days to go through the list and assess all the top talent and their potential development paths. This assessment process is currently projected out to the year 2010.

4. Once these potential leaders are identified, they become part of an extensive mentoring program that is cross-functional in nature. For example, Simpson might be mentoring one of the next presidents of foreign operations, while Bill Carroll, the current president of the Automotive Systems Group, might be mentoring the next CFO.

5. The succession program also reaches below the top leadership positions through the company's Global Management Resources Program. According to Simpson, "We have a database and it is all there. We know who everyone is and have a complete inventory for each individual in the company. Behind every senior financial individual, operating individual, support individual—for example, human resources or legal—there are three or four names. These people are all long-term Dana executives, with high-octane potential. It is all part of our rite of passage."

In implementing Dana's succession planning and evaluating its effectiveness, Simpson notes, a number of factors come into play. First, the company works very hard at getting the right matches: "getting the right people, in the right places, doing the right things, and at the right time." The company claims its success rate is very good primarily because the company's turnover rate is very low and tenure very high.

Also, the company's organizational structure helps to facilitate these right matches. Essentially, a two-dimensional matrix integrates its core businesses and regional locations. Each core business has a product parent or senior executive responsible for overseeing design, development, and production processes. Also, each region has its own president responsible for dealing with customers, finding new markets, and defining strategic opportunities. This two-dimensional matrix approach facilitates cross-functional communication at the company, such as on-site meetings, video conferencing, and e-mail, and it leads to a broader knowledge and awareness of the talent that exists throughout the organization.

Leadership Qualities: Taking Inventory

When Simpson speaks about "taking an inventory of a person," what are some of the key leadership qualities he looks for? During his interview, he highlighted some of these qualities. (Figure 6.2 offers more of Simpson's thoughts on leadership.)

First, given the company's emphasis on experiential learning and the importance it places on an international assignment, it should not be surprising that one important leadership quality is mobility. According to Simpson, mobility is important because it is indicative of a person's willingness to change. If a person is not willing to change, then how is the company going to give that person the experiences he or she needs to develop—or to be evaluated as—a leader? Certainly, reluctance to change is going to be a significant limiting factor in the ability to take on leadership challenges and responsibilities.

Simpson recounts such a situation when he first took the CFO position in 1997. A person reporting to Simpson was in his early forties, had a couple of children, and was concerned about preserving the balance between his work and family life. Simpson spoke to him about controller positions in Europe and Asia, but when the time came to take action, Simpson could not get him to go on the interviews. Essentially, according to Simpson, he just did not want to leave the country and shake up his family life. Simpson notes, "Nevertheless, we found a good match for him at the company. Not one leading from downstairs to upstairs but in a different functional direction. The individual is still moving—although not in the direction we would have liked to see him headed. But time will tell. He had the wherewithal, was a good employee—10 to 12 years of experience—and we did not want to lose him. At Dana, the cream rises to the top. There's no great secret to leadership development. There's no mathematical equation. But there's lots of psychology involved."

This example and related observations give rise to modulation, the second quality of leadership. What is modulation? According to Simpson, "It is the process whereby one moves between the softness

Figure 6.2
John (Jack) S. Simpson
Former Executive Vice President and CFO
Thoughts on Leadership

Throughout the interviews at Dana, we were pleased to hear many views about leadership, leadership development, and the importance of the Dana Style. While most of these thoughts have been incorporated into the case study, the following ideas on leadership are a useful addendum. We greatly appreciate both the sincerity and candor in which these quotes were offered to us.

■ Leadership starts with a vision. One needs to know where the company is going—such as the tactics that need to be employed to achieve its strategic goals. Whether it is the CFO or a business unit controller, we should all be the right arm of our respective bosses.

■ There is a lot of soft stuff at this company—but at the end of the day we are a numbers- and shareholder-driven company.

■ Part of being a leader is to listen—and a good leader listens. What do you think? What would you change? How would you change it? And they will tell you! *Leadership Secrets of Attila the Hun*—the best book that I ever read on leadership—because he was a great listener and his followers connected with him because he listened and he absorbed and he assimilated.

■ There are a variety of leadership skills. Some are innate and some you have to acquire. Managers do things right while leaders do the right things. That's the difference! Doing the right things means you are conquering. You are Attila. You are a warrior taking market share away from your enemies.

■ Incumbent upon a good leader is to spot the values and the strengths that each individual carries within them and try to help them self-actualize (i.e., to become even a greater asset to both themselves and the company). As a leader, I don't think you discard or ignore anyone. I think you hone. What I look for is a good, solid, honest person with integrity, fire in the belly, and a fit within the Dana Style.

■ Today, for a global company, the CFO's job is the toughest job in corporate America. It's the most complex and most demanding. You must be a tactician, strategist, and a motivator. A leader is all of that. By the time you go home at night, expect to be punch-drunk.

■ Why, as leaders, do we go to the plants, the divisions, and business units? Sure, to look at the plants, to look at how they are treating our customers, to look at throughput, to look at cycle time, and the capital productivity. But first and foremost we are there to take an inventory of our people.

and hardness of the Dana Style. Business reality is found somewhere in between these forces and it is at that point you are most likely going to come to the right solution for the company." The example noted above is a case in point. Simpson respected the man for saying no, but his decision definitely had the effect of slowing his career path for exhibiting these competencies in the organization.

Finally, Simpson emphasized the importance of teamwork. In the past, teamwork at Dana was largely an outgrowth of common military experience. Simpson served in Vietnam, and he points out that today most of the members of the policy committee have served in the military. He notes, "If you want to learn about character, personality, and discipline, the military will do that for you, more than your parents, more than school, more than anything. If you screw up, they are going to fix you real quick. You are going to learn and be disciplined for it and you will be better off for it, both in the short and long run."

Simpson continues,

Self-control is very important for effective leadership. You have to learn it. You have to learn how to control your tongue and emotions and use them at the right time. It is self-discipline. You have to learn the difference when you can, and when you can't, say something, and that's really the edge of the razor. If you say the wrong things to the wrong individual you are going to have disharmony, disruptions, and so forth, and things are going to break down. This discipline becomes even more important as you move up in the organization because your actions impact even more people.

Simpson concludes,

There are some companies that are going to say "Hogwash to the soft stuff. Just give me the guy who can put the numbers on the board." But in our company there must be that Dana Style and demonstrated modulation. Treat your people with respect, honesty, integrity, and most important, listen. We view it all as our secret competitive weapon.

Given the value placed on military experience, one might wonder what would take the place of such experience in the future. In this regard, Rothlisberger offers a few suggestions on the qualities he looks for when bringing on new members of the audit staff.

One is a background in school activities, especially sports. He has generally found that when individuals express themselves well, which is an important quality for today's financial executive, the chances are that they were involved in team activities. He notes, "It seems like the individuals that rise to the top have played volleyball or softball or soccer. I don't know for sure, but maybe such activities give someone a sense of teamwork, a sense of winning and losing, so that even if you should lose, you know that the sun will come up tomorrow. It just seems that these activities give people the confidence they need to keep trying in the face of adversity."

On the theme of confidence, Rothlisberger says,

A good number of the people we have hired are from smaller towns or colleges. Again, I can't say for sure, but it seems that when coming from such places, these individuals have a sense or feeling that as a person you can do things and make a difference. This thinking seems to follow them in their careers. For example, an individual's first plant controller assignment for this company may only be as large as a rounding error; nevertheless, these people seem to understand that you can still make a difference and that you don't have to accept the way things have always been.

Dana University

There is no formal leadership training at Dana. No one takes a course to become a leader. Nor does Dana typically hire its leaders from the outside. Instead, leadership development is ingrained into the Dana Style. Leadership development is encouraged and facilitated through experiential learning, a policy that emphasizes promotion from within, based on performance, and a long history of succession planning that goes back to the company's founders.

Nevertheless, internal training plays a large part in Dana's way of doing things. It goes back to the theme of total involvement and participation. In fact, through Dana University, its on-site educational facility, the company now offers its employees hundreds of course offerings ranging from technical business subjects and customer problem-solving workshops to important areas of personal improvement such as effective presentation skills and how to develop one's personal strengths for effective management.

Each year, between two and three thousand Dana employees attend Dana University programs. Those who are interested can also earn a fully accredited MBA or an MS in engineering. Although the university uses some outside resources to help develop courses and workshop materials, a staff of full-time Dana University trainers delivers and conducts the programs. Worldwide, this staff includes almost 150 full- and part-time trainers located at both Dana University in Toledo, Ohio, and at the plant levels. These trainers are frequently assisted by Dana employees who take a large part in role-playing exercises as well as serving as course facilitators in technical areas.

Although the courses the university offers are too numerous to list here, one aspect of the curriculum is especially relevant to our discussion: Dana University's Manager Certification Program. This program consists of six courses, four of which directly touch on the behavioral competencies emphasized in this research.

1. How to Develop Your Personal Strengths for Effective Managing

2. How to Use Supervisory Skills to Get Results

3. Developing the 9, 9 Style of Managing

4. Problem Solving/Decision Making

5. Product Cost Analysis for Non-Financial People

6. Financial Planning for Business Success

After completing these six courses, a Dana employee is certified as a manager. This certification is considered very important at the company. There is no formal requirement that it be completed, but it is well understood that manager certification is one of the items considered when examining the list of so-called promotables. Duncan James notes, "In the past 25 years, I have probably seen every controller in the company go through this certification process."

For finance people, certification generally occurs around the same time they are assigned their first plant controller assignment, about five or six years after joining the firm. It is interesting to note that there are no grades or pass/fails for these programs. The only requirement is to attend the programs and participate. This is consistent with the Dana Style.

In addition to the programs at Dana University, employees are free to meet the 40 hours of training per year expected of them in a number of other ways. For example, the Dana recently hosted an in-house a leadership program run by professors from the University of Michigan. This program was directed at some of the company's midlevel managers. Also, James notes that it is becoming increasingly popular to send many of the more senior executives off for a week or two to one of the advanced management programs offered by some of the more prestigious universities.

There is no formal HR department involved in career development and training at Dana University. While HR plays a larger role in these matters at the plant level, most of the HR function at Dana is concerned with compliance and diversity issues. According to James, "There is no HR person at Dana for finance. Here HR is more administrative and is less engaged in training and development. However, they are certainly involved in recommending people for different positions and opportunities within the company and we highly value their input."

Concerning the future role of Dana University, a few concluding observations are worth emphasizing, according to Duncan James:

> Dana University is even more important today than ever before. Given our growth and expansion pressures, the university gives us a platform to spread the Dana Style—both through the core management courses and simply due to the fact that you are meeting a lot of people from other parts of the company. I think one of the great benefits you get when attending a Dana University program is the experience you obtain working with other people as much as the course content itself.

And, Rothlisberger adds,

> We do a lot of training here at Dana. When we first introduced Excellence in Manufacturing (EIM), we were talking about lower inventory levels, what it takes to get them, as well as talking about things like line throughput time, zero setup, and zero scrap. These

were all new things on the manufacturing side that had to change if you were going to get your inventories down and still be able to meet customer demand. We used Dana University to do a lot of that training. In the future, we see more training being directed at a specific plant or a specific division, so we need a common group setting allowing us to get together to solve a problem. Training at Dana University has become more focused on problem solving and has become more integrated into our business strategy. It's part of the Dana Style.

James sums up,

People skills are the most important for finance people today and that's what the certification helps provide them with. There is a lot of teamwork and group/self assessment built into these courses, and that includes the two finance programs as well. But moving people around must reinforce this training. Here at Dana you have to make a lot of lateral moves before you move up the ladder. However, when we speak of people skills at Dana we use the words, "cross fertilization." People move across disciplines not so much to master them as to manage them. Dana people communicate through their experiences. It is simply the Dana Style of doing things.

Endnotes

1. Since this interview, and before this case study was published, Simpson retired from Dana Corporation.

2. Simpson highly recommends Micheline Maynard's book, *The Global Manufacturing Vanguard: New Rules From the Industry Elite* (New York: John Wiley & Sons, 1998). See the annotated bibliography for further details on this reference.

Nortel Networks Corporation

Company Background

Nortel Networks Corporation (Nortel Networks) is a global supplier of communications networks and services for data and telephony. As a result of Nortel Networks' $6.9 billion acquisition of Bay Networks, Inc., in 1998, it became the largest company in Canada.[1] With 1998 revenues of $17.6 billion, Nortel Networks has approximately 70,000 employees across 150 countries and territories.

Approximately four years ago, CFO Frank Dunn requested an initiative to promote leadership development for finance employees. This request reflects a commitment at the highest levels of finance at Nortel Networks to develop its people. It also highlights a corporate culture in which finance plays an important role as a strategic business partner.

Accordingly, finance has been at the forefront of leadership development at Nortel Networks, recently culminating in an award-winning competency-based development initiative. At Nortel Networks, finance has taken competency development in a more objective, explicit, and measurable direction.

Financial Leadership at Nortel Networks

Katherine Parker formerly the senior advisor,[2] change management, human resources, for global finance says, "There is an enormous amount of pride in being part of finance at Nortel Networks. Finance people are not 'bean counters.' They are valued members of the organization. They have strong business acumen and are business solution people." Carl Marcotte, director of credit management, echoes those sentiments: "The finance function is well integrated with the business function.

Finance cuts across all business units at Nortel Networks. The role of finance has become markedly more complex, corresponding with the vast increase in the complexity of the business. There's always been a focus on 'how can we make ourselves more valuable to the business?'—a professional pride that finance is going to help the organization."

Parker added, "We have given the business a number of successful general managers. If senior executives are looking for a general manager to head up a line of business, they often look toward our finance executives. Overall, there's a great deal of respect for finance in the organization."

In an interesting example of finance as "business solution people," Nortel Networks has taken the initiative to finance some of its customers, allowing them to purchase and construct new telecommunication networks services that they might otherwise have been unable to finance. Such a win-win solution involves much complexity at a number of levels and underscores the strategic place of finance in the organization. Kate Stevenson, treasurer of Nortel Networks, views Nortel's customer financing expertise and capability as "a powerful competitive weapon which finance can use as a key differentiating factor to win new business." In short, she sees this as an example of how finance and the business work together as partners to offer winning solutions to their customers.

Moreover, finance and HR associates, supported at the highest levels of the company, understand that being a strategic partner with a place at the business table, as opposed to a bean counter, calls for interpersonal and intrapersonal competencies—leverage competencies.

The following sections describe competency-based leadership development processes in Nortel Network's finance function. Figure 7.1 diagrams and summarizes the central processes discussed here. It may be useful to refer to this diagram while reading this case study.

A Benchmark Initiative: Mapping Your Future (MYF)

Katherine Parker was hired as a full-time change management expert. Her responsibility was to develop and implement the leadership development initiative desired by the CFO. She built a design team consisting of eight HR and 11 finance associate volunteers from 10 locations. To

Figure 7.1
Major Processes Involved in Competency-Based Finance Employee
Development at Nortel

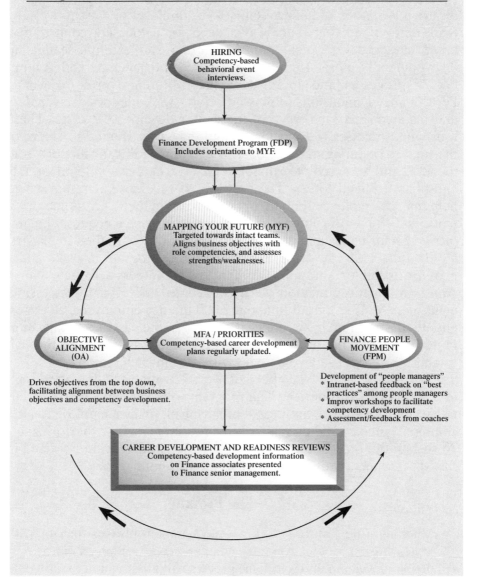

ensure that the program would meet the needs of all finance employees, each regional finance location had an opportunity to include a representative on the team.[3]

After carefully assessing and identifying career development gaps at different levels across finance (entry level, midlevel, and executive), the team determined that there was a need for a focused, competency-based career development model. Internal and external leadership development best practices were researched and benchmarked. A number of processes and tools, most incorporating Nortel Networks' Performance Dimensions (discussed below), were identified, evaluated, and mapped into each stage of the career development cycle. These tools and processes were validated and tested on about 30 percent of the finance population. In January 1998, after significant support from the CFO and his executive cabinet to focus on career development, HR and finance joined forces. The goal was to develop a plan that would help finance employees enhance performance in their current jobs, prepare them for future jobs, and respond to employee requests for improved performance and development discussions with their managers.

By June 1998, the team had a structured program in place and a plan for its implementation. Two hundred volunteers across the North American finance function were trained to deliver a three-session, eight-hour MYF program to about 2,000 finance employees. To differentiate this program from others attempted in the past and to fully integrate it into the finance culture, the program was delivered through established teams using volunteer facilitators in each region.

By early 1999, MYF had been delivered to almost all finance associates across North America.[4] The program will eventually be rolled out to Europe and Asia, with the goal of having all finance employees use a common language to discuss career development and performance. To sustain the program into the future, all new hires will be trained in the MYF process within their first six months in finance.

MYF: The Program

Mapping Your Future is a career development process that integrates business objectives and competency development into a people development cycle. This process will assist you in identifying your business goals and the links to your specific core performance dimensions, and accurate people development plans. The outcome will be a detailed, integrated people development plan for your department.[5]

The MYF program consists of five steps. The first three involve facilitators delivering a program divided into three sessions of one, two, and five hours, respectively. The fourth and fifth steps involve discussions between managers and employees following up on the program and implementing a career development plan (figure 7.2).

Step 1 is a meeting between the facilitator and the team manager. The manager is introduced to the MYF process.

Step 2 is a prework session introducing the whole team to the process and the tools involved. It also allows the facilitator to become familiar with the team, troubleshoot any potential problems, and tailor the workshop to the needs of the team.

Step 3 is a five-hour workshop. It involves identifying business objectives and linking those objectives to the team members' roles and skill sets (competencies). Team members are oriented toward competencies, reach a consensus on the 12 key competencies necessary for the performance of their roles, and determine their level of mastery of each of these competencies and what their strengths and weaknesses are.

Following the workshop, participants begin a personal development plan. Participants are also provided the book *Career Anchors*,[6] as recommended reading which describes priorities and values and how those values relate to career choices. This helps people frame a larger, long-term perspective. Methods of competency development are outlined to help individuals close the gaps in their behavioral skills.

In steps 4 and 5, managers and employees further analyze competency gaps and complete a career development plan.

An attempt is made to be as objective and behaviorally based as possible. A number of competency-based tools are used in the MYF program. The backbone of these is the *Performance Dimensions Development Map*,[7] developed through the Nortel Networks Learning Institute. Nortel Networks describes Performance Dimensions as follows:

Figure 7.2
Mapping Your Future ("MYF")

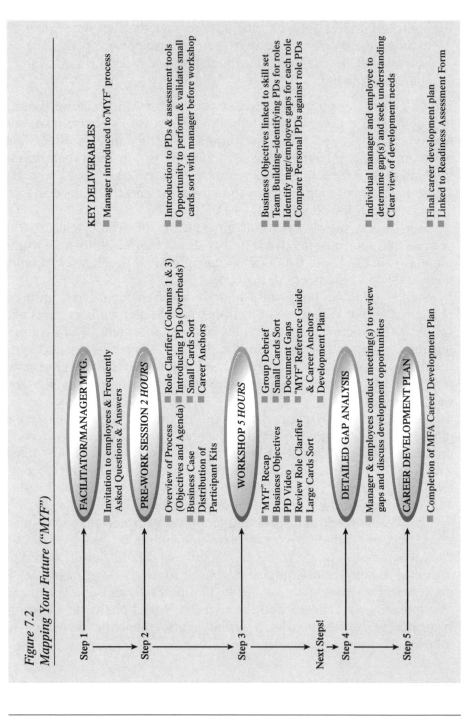

FACILITATOR/MANAGER MTG.

Step 1

- Invitation to employees & Frequently Asked Questions & Answers

KEY DELIVERABLES
- Manager introduced to "MYF" process

PRE-WORK SESSION 2 HOURS

Step 2

- Overview of Process (Objectives and Agenda)
- Business Case
- Distribution of Participant Kits
- Role Clarifier (Columns 1 & 3)
- Introducing PDs (Overheads)
- Small Cards Sort
- Career Anchors

- Introduction to PDs & assessment tools
- Opportunity to perform & validate small cards sort with manager before workshop

WORKSHOP 5 HOURS

Step 3

- "MYF" Recap
- Business Objectives
- PD Video
- Review Role Clarifier
- Large Cards Sort
- Group Debrief
- Small Cards Sort
- Document Gaps
- "MYF" Reference Guide & Career Anchors
- Development Plan

- Business Objectives linked to skill set
- Team Building–identifying PDs for roles
- Identify mgr/employee gaps for each role
- Compare Personal PDs against role PDs

Next Steps!

DETAILED GAP ANALYSIS

Step 4

- Manager & employees conduct meeting(s) to review gaps and discuss development opportunities

- Individual manager and employee to determine gap(s) and seek understanding
- Clear view of development needs

CAREER DEVELOPMENT PLAN

Step 5

- Completion of MFA Career Development Plan

- Final career development plan
- Linked to Readiness Assessment Form

Performance Dimensions are synonymous with competencies, sometimes also referred to as core competencies. At Nortel Networks we say:

"Performance Dimension competencies are a set of measurable performance criteria to enable Nortel Networks employees to understand the professional 'on the job' behaviors that they can display to improve their performance and therefore the chances of success in the company. Hence they are called Performance Dimensions. Each dimension is described at four levels, where level one is the most basic, and level four is the highest level of complexity."

Each of these dimensions or competencies describes skills that an employee needs to have in order to do his/her job effectively, such as Teamwork, Relationship Building, or Judgment. There are also technical/professional skills that are specific to each job or role. Not all competencies are required in every role and not always at the same level of mastery. The key to this process is in understanding what competencies are required in a given role and to what extent and how an employee "fits" within that role profile. The process of assessing employees' "fit" is made more objective by focusing only on demonstrated behaviors, using specific examples of how an employee operates day-to-day across all of these dimensions or competencies. Notice we did not say the process is completely objective. We said it is more objective. Managing human beings will never be a completely objective process.[8]

The *Performance Dimensions Development Map* includes 22 Performance Dimensions (PDs). They were created from multiple competency models used in Nortel Networks, interviews with executives on needs for future skill sets, and with the assistance of an established international consulting firm. The MYF design team, along with senior finance management, refined the list to 12 core competencies thought to be most important to leadership in the finance function. They represent the behaviors on which finance would like its leaders to be focusing. Figure 7.3 lists and defines sample PDs.

Figure 7.3
Sample Performance Dimensions

Change Management/Adaptability. The ability to maintain effectiveness in a changing environment.

Developing Others. The ability to foster the learning and development of other people with an appropriate level of needs analysis, coaching, and other support.

Influence. The ability to persuade or influence other people to accept a point of view, adopt a specific agenda, or take a course of action.

Listening and Responding. The ability to accurately listen to others—understanding their feelings, needs, and points of view—and then respond appropriately.

Team Leadership. The ability to take a role as leader of a team or other group. It involves taking action to increase the motivation of all team members to achieve business goals.

Source: *Performance Dimensions Development Map,* 4–5.

In the following discussion, the MYF design team explains that analysis and customer orientation were not selected as among the top 12 core competencies because they are givens. The discussion also highlights the importance of developing one's own role profile and performance dimensions on which to focus:

> The reason analysis is not one of the top 12 is that it represents what we refer to as "table stakes" (it is "a given"). We would not expect our leaders to be focusing on analysis because they should have already developed that skill to the level necessary to get them to a leadership position. Obviously, in order to maximize performance in an analyst role, analysis may show up in your development plan as one of the top PDs on which you need to focus. Once you have developed to the point where you are covering all critical areas required by your role, demonstrating a few of the top 12 finance PDs will begin to differentiate you from your peers and set you apart as one demonstrating skills we are looking for in future leaders.

> Customer orientation's omission is similar to analysis. There is no clear differentiation between the customer orientation of someone just starting their career and someone in a senior leadership posi-

tion in finance. Because finance is a support function, none of us will be successful unless we make customer orientation a "table stakes" competency. That is why customer orientation was not included in the top 12—it is a given. It MUST happen before we can do almost anything else.

One way to look at this is if either analysis or customer orientation were included in the top 12 leadership competencies, it would say that we want our leaders concentrating on those PDs for their development. The expectation is that our leaders have already developed both analysis and customer orientation to the required level for their roles.

Note, however, that there are no table stakes when it comes to doing your own role profile. If a behavior is critical for success in your role, that behavior should be in your role profile. The key is narrowing your focus to concentrate on the most critical behaviors.[9]

The discussion goes on to make a similar point regarding technical finance skills:

All employees need to focus on developing BOTH technical skills and behavioral skills. The Mapping Your Future workshop is intended to focus on behavioral aspects, but in no way should you assume that technical skills are less important to your long-term success than behavioral skills. Finance requires a technical skills foundation, and we have been historically successful in developing technical skills in our people. We have not focused as much on behavioral skills in the past, which is the fundamental difference between this initiative and previous ones. In our quest to become a world-class finance organization, we need to balance our focus on technical AND behavioral skills.[10]

The competencies outlined in the *Performance Dimensions Development Map* are used in MYF workshop exercises designed to help people develop role profiles, identify the top 12 performance dimensions that are most critical to success in their job, identify their strengths and development needs in relation to critical PDs and priorities, and identify the differences between manager and employee on some of these perceptions and findings.

The *Performance Dimensions Development Map* identifies and defines competencies at four different levels, as noted earlier, and provides "exemplary behaviors" at each level, as well as "developmental activities," which are recommendations for developing competencies at each level. It also offers recommended readings and programs designed to assist in skills development.

Ultimately, a detailed career development plan is created after thorough discussions with supervisors. Follow-up discussions and evaluations at various points throughout the year continue the work on competency development. According to Parker, "Experience is the teacher." That is, while formal training is available, the emphasis for the development of competencies is on providing growth experiences. For example, an individual who needs work on team building may be given the responsibility of leading a team. His or her progress on developing this skill would be monitored and reinforced by the supervisor.

Integrating MYF

The principles of MYF are being integrated into the finance culture, in part by becoming embedded within existing processes and mechanisms, including hiring and development processes. Follow-up programs for finance, designed to further the implementation of MYF goals and principles, have been developed, and are discussed below.

Finance Development Program (FDP)

FDP is a program for new hires in finance at Nortel Networks. According to Parker, "FDP invites all nonmanagement, nonclerical new hires to participate with the promise that it will expedite their professional development for the first three years of their career." The program is run by an FDP committee made up of FDP participants and an HR advisor. Participants are encouraged to rotate through a number of development assignments in Nortel Networks to ensure breadth and depth of experience. They are invited to attend an FDP leadership development conference for each of the three years. "Through such conferences," says Parker, "new hires network and socialize all over the world." Top executives speak to them on various topics, and participants interact in subteams and projects. Participants are introduced to MYF principles and procedures at the conferences. Parker noted that

John Roth, CEO of Nortel Networks, holds up FDP as a benchmark orientation/development model for Nortel Networks. This is due, in large part, to its "inclusive, not exclusive" philosophy.

All new hires are oriented through FDP. It is worthwhile to note that assessment of performance dimensions—that is, competencies—for finance associates begins before they start to work at Nortel Networks. Behavioral event job interview guides have been developed based on a *Performance Dimensions Dictionary.*[11] Key PDs and mastery levels needed for success in a given job in finance are outlined. Further, the PDs are listed in the job profile, so a job candidate can consider whether he or she is a good fit for the role and anticipate the questions an interviewer might ask.[12]

Managing for Achievement (MFA) and Priorities

Managing for Achievement (MFA) is the performance review process of Nortel Networks. It involves meeting with one's manager on a quarterly basis and receiving yearly ratings. Job purposes, key responsibilities, and key customers are outlined. Performance objectives are delineated, including operating, development, and business objectives. Operating objectives are defined as those that connect directly to the implementation of the business plan, budget, and department plans. People development objectives enhance the capabilities, skills, and future contributions of people and teams. Strengthening the business objectives are steps that will position the business for greater competitive and operational strength in the future. The objectives are made as specific and measurable as possible.

An assessment is made of the employee's strengths and areas requiring additional emphasis, and a development plan is outlined. The plan includes development focus, actions planned, application to the job, and status/timing. The company recommends that employees and managers use PDs in completing the assessment and development plan.

Nortel Networks has updated the MFA process to make it even more behavioral/competency based. The process is now called "Priorities."

Priorities is a program designed for both project teams and individuals. It focuses on results and how to achieve them. Development discussions occur continuously throughout the year and involve ongoing dialogue and feedback. *Priorities FAQs* [frequently asked questions][13] provide more comprehensive feedback to employees by:

- Setting expectations on results, how to achieve results, productivity enablers, development and feedback up front in functional or project roles.

- Providing a way for employees to capture ongoing feedback from several sources—avoiding surprises at project or period closeout.

- Capturing and presenting performance feedback and evaluation on two dimensions critical to performance—outcomes and behaviors.

Nortel maintains an ongoing feedback graph, tracking progress on both outcome and behaviors. In explaining the term "behaviors," *Priorities FAQs* states that it's "about developing ways of working at Nortel Networks that will contribute to our sustained success. Performance Dimensions (PDs) can help you think about how you achieve your results. PDs are definitions of on-the-job behaviors demonstrated by effective Nortel Networks employees and managers."

Thus, both results and the way one achieves results will be evaluated. How much weight each of these dimensions will hold will be determined by employees and their managers. Both the functional manager (the manager who maintains an ongoing relationship with the employee) and the project manager are involved in this process. Feedback comes from a variety of sources, including peers. Training in Priorities, including classroom and computer-based training, is available to employees.

Career Development Readiness Reviews

Along with performance evaluations and development planning, each regional finance council reviews finance employees in terms of their readiness for a development move. According to Parker, "Before the evolution of our open, honest dialogue concept using competencies, the councils gathered the data, then the chairs of the councils would get together and spend all day reviewing 100 people or more." Many perceived the process as being too secretive and leaving too much room for subjectivity.

This process was modified to make it more of a review and to provide competency definitions and other criteria that eliminate some of the personal judgment. Now all regions examine and discuss the development of finance employees using consistent, reliable criteria to guide the conversation. There are still regional finance council meetings to keep track of employees' development, but MYF concepts have been incorporated into the structure of what are now more aptly called career development and readiness reviews. A finance employee's development data are reviewed by each manager and then recorded by regional councils for use in succession planning.

MYF: Status

With MYF, finance at Nortel Networks has taken the lead in integrating competencies into the language and culture of the organization. As Parker noted, "It was a cultural sweep." While PDs have been available to all Nortel Networks employees since about 1995, finance has taken the lead in competency modeling by weaving it into the fabric of the function. From new-hire interviewing and orientation to career development, 360-degree feedback mechanisms, and succession planning, finance employees have fully embedded PDs into their employee development lexicon.

The MYF workshops will not be repeated annually. According to Parker, "Now they have the learning, they have the context, they have the materials. It's not the training that will cause change, it's what participants do with the training that will make the difference. The team dialogues will continue. They have the model and the direction." There is a new hires' handbook—a self-directed MYF. Every new hire will work with his or her manager on role definition, competencies, and developing a competency-based growth plan.

Parker emphasizes that

MYF isn't the answer. It's a facilitator and is meant to empower individuals to chart their own course. The main principle of MYF is to facilitate open, honest dialogue between managers and employees about career development. MYF embeds all the career development tools we use in Nortel Networks. It's up to the individual and his or her manager to sustain it. It's up to individuals to hold themselves accountable for using that or anything else.

MYF is a continuous career development process mapped out in the following five steps:[14]

1. *Where Am I?* This involves self-observation and generating a vision.

2. *Assess the Various Routes.* Understand your current role and assess yourself against the required skill set.

3. *Chart Your Course.* Identify the actions and support required to develop the skills.

4. *Find Your Way.* Practice, reinforce, and record your development.

5. *Use Your Results.* Ensure that results become an integral part of work life for employees and managers.

Regarding the high level of acceptance of MYF among finance employees, Parker says, "The key was engaging a number of stakeholders. There has been a groundswell of appreciation for it. I've actually had managers come to me and say 'I live and breathe MYF.'" She notes, however, that not all employees have embraced it, and there is still much work to be done. Stevenson says, "By and large, it has taken hold. We need to make it part of our everyday thinking."

Such a statement reflects the support for MYF principles at the highest levels of finance and is a testament to the hard work that has gone into this initiative. In fact, Parker accepted the 1998 Finance Award of Excellence on behalf of the MYF design team in recognition of outstanding achievement in the category of employee value.

Beyond MYF: Further Initiatives

The company has begun to implement initiatives that support and complement MYF. They include Objective Alignment and the Finance People Movement (FPM).

Objective Alignment

As noted above, an integral part of MYF involves identifying business objectives and aligning them with team members' roles. Nortel found that this process needed strengthening. "Developing in and of itself is very good," Parker says, "but out of context it's meaningless to the business. So what we're doing now is another initiative called Objective Alignment. This is an offshoot of MYF. It is a structured way of driving objectives from the top down. It starts with the CEO and the CFO."

In this process, objectives cascade from the CEO to the CFO and business president to finance teams and, ultimately, individuals. The goal is to have SMART objectives: specific, measurable, actionable, realistic, and time bound.[15]

Parker says, "Once the CFO delineates and aligns his objectives with the CEO's, then there is a solid set of objectives for the function which is mapped to our business. This exercise equips employees with a solid business focus. These objectives are then used by each group to identify high- and low-priority actions and areas that are critical to the overall success of Nortel Networks."

The Finance People Movement

Finance's next people development initiative focuses on the development of the subgroup of people managers at Nortel Networks. These are managers from the middle level to just below the executive level. The subgroup also includes finance employees who manage people today or may manage people in the foreseeable future and employees who supervise others or lead teams. The initiative takes on the qualities of a movement rather than a program. It looks to facilitate ongoing dialogue and feedback between and among managers and nonmanagers. Twenty people from across North America—17 finance associates and three HR associates—volunteered to join the FPM team.

Finance employees are invited to participate in three "waves of excitement." Wave One has already been rolled out. Finance employees in five regions were surveyed to determine the qualities they considered essential for a good people manager. Individuals and teams were encouraged to contribute their ideas in fun and creative ways, for example, in the form of poems and songs. The material sent to employees informed them that:

> The team will present your feedback to the finance executive cabinet, and to the Regional Finance councils. The information we gather will also be used to complete additional materials we can use in Mapping Your Future to increase self-awareness about how behavior impacts productivity and job satisfaction. The experiences,

key events, and behaviors you describe will form the stories we need to tell to support *Growth and Development in Finance,* among other things.

The description of what makes an excellent people manager was placed on the FPM Web site.

Wave One: Communicate and Talk involves reviewing this input, giving feedback, and providing more examples on the Web site under "Best Practices."

Wave Two: Do Something Different was rolled out in fall 1999. All finance employees were invited to participate in a workshop called PD Improv. The FPM team designed a PD Improv town hall that incorporates a highly interactive module that teaches improvisation techniques. A trained, working actor and improvisation master was hired to deliver this interactive workshop to hundreds of finance associates simultaneously. It focused on the development of listening and communication skills and the importance of teammates. No notes needed to be taken during this fun, experiential, memorable workshop. Three hundred employees participated in the pilot program, which, according to Parker, received outstanding reviews.

Wave Three: PD Improv Workshop for Managers will be offered to all mid-level managers in finance. The workshop will be implemented region by region by a trained set of coaches from HR and finance. In preparation for the workshop, each participant will be asked to complete a Managing for Success self-evaluation and begin a 360-degree feedback performance dimension-based survey.

After the 360-degree survey period (about two weeks), participants will attend a five-hour workshop in which coaches take them through their feedback and help them shape it into manageable priorities for 2000. Parker says, "Through [the workshop] they develop their personal development objectives. Again, that feeds into priorities/MFA." Participants will receive a PD Improv Certificate, adding to the momentum of the movement through branding.

Thus, a largely competency-based leadership development movement, dovetailing with MYF and supported by a variety of tools, mechanisms, and structures, is in the process of being embedded in finance at Nortel Networks.

Executive Leadership Development

While many top-level Nortel Networks finance executives have been involved with or have supported MYF in different capacities (e.g., as speakers or by setting objectives), there are separate initiatives targeted at evaluating and developing the leadership attributes of this group. Every year, John Roth holds a leadership review of all his direct reports, including the CFO. For this review, he developed a list of leadership attributes, described by Parker:

> We have a 360 [degree feedback] tool that helps measure these leadership attributes. And the expectation is that each of these executives will be going through development dialogues with their managers and trying to grow those six leadership attributes. All of our finance executives are going to be going through this 360-degree leadership review. HR is building an executive coaching capability in preparation for that review so that we have trained executive coaches who can work with the executives one-on-one. That is how we're going to accelerate the development of this group.

Parker notes that finance executives have certain specialized needs such as "having the capacity to stay calm in the throes of chaos. Large divestitures, mergers, etc., require hard emotional decisions. You need to be unflappable." Individualized executive coaching may be helpful in addressing such issues. Thus, Nortel expects that more individualized leadership development opportunities will also be available to executives at the highest levels of finance.

Conclusions

Figure 7.1 diagrams and summarizes processes involved in competency-based development at Nortel Networks. The process begins at the hiring level, through the use of behavioral event interviews. FDP includes orientations to competencies and MYF for all nonmanagement, nonclerical new hires; thus, MYF and FDP complement each other. MYF takes a central position, as it represents a complete career development process. MYF, Objective Alignment, and FPM feed back into one another.

Priorities also takes a central position, as it records the dialogues between managers and employees in ongoing career development plans and reviews. These data are also recorded in a regional career readiness review, further reinforcing the importance of competencies for finance associates.

Parker recalls that she was initially advised not to use the term "competency" because it was considered "too HR." That competency development has been accepted in finance is clear, since the term is now part of the language of finance at Nortel. Finance has also developed a wheel of guiding values and principles that reinforces the need to balance people and performance and emphasizes rewarding the right competencies and behaviors.

Thus, by consistently, deliberately charting the course for employee growth over a period of three years, the finance function of Nortel Networks has taken the lead in integrating competency-based development into its culture. It has done so through a group of creative and complementary initiatives and by using existing tools and mechanisms. It has also had support from the highest levels of finance.

Summary

- Finance at Nortel Networks is a valued strategic partner to the business.

- The role of finance has become markedly more complex, corresponding to the ever-increasing complexity of the business.

- The expanding strategic role of finance calls for a greater focus on the development of leverage competencies.

- An initiative was rolled out called Mapping Your Future. It is an award-winning initiative that involves aligning business objectives and role performance dimensions (competencies) and assessing personal strengths and weaknesses against those dimensions. The outcome is a detailed integrated development plan for each department and its staff.

- MYF is an ongoing process, not an event. Existing corporate structures and mechanisms are used to ensure continued dialogue between manager and employee on competency development.

- Another initiative, Objective Alignment, is being rolled out to strengthen the alignment between business objectives and Performance Dimensions. Such an alignment is critical to providing a context for competency development.

- A Finance People Movement has been initiated to focus on the development of managers. Using creative, engaging tools and workshops, it is a grassroots movement that feeds back into MYF.

- A key element in successfully integrating competency development into finance has been the involvement of key finance stakeholders in the process.

- It is expected that in the future, executives at the highest levels of finance at Nortel Networks will participate in competency-based leadership development programs.

- Competency development in finance at Nortel Networks is seen as a continuous, life-long learning process.

Endnotes

1. Nortel Networks 1998 Annual Report. For more information about the company, visit its Web site at www.nortelnetworks.com.

2. Katherine Parker has been promoted to Director, Business Effectiveness, Service Enabling Solutions, Nortel Networks, since the time of this interview.

3. This and much of the following description are taken from the Mapping Your Future Award of Excellence Nomination Form.

4. While the program was not specifically delivered to the approximately 60 top finance executives, known as the Executive Management Team (EMT), many of these executives were involved with the program in various capacities, and their leadership development will be discussed below.

5. *Mapping Your Future: A Reference Guide for Developing Employees in Global Finance* (Nortel Networks, June 1998).

6. E. H. Schein, *Career Anchors: Discovering Your Real Values,* rev. ed. (San Francisco: Jossey-Bass/Pfeiffer, 1993).

7. Performance Dimensions Development Map, Version 3 (Nortel Networks Learning Institute, Nortel Networks).

8. More Frequently Asked Questions and Answers About Mapping Your Future (Nortel Networks, 1999), 3.

9. Ibid., 4–5.

10. Ibid., 7.

11. *Performance Dimensions Dictionary* (Nortel Networks Learning Institute, Nortel Networks).

12. Ibid., 9.

13. *Priorities FAQs* (Nortel Networks, July 17, 1999), 1.

14. *Mapping Your Future.*

15. *Priorities FAQs, 3.*

8

Solvay Polymers, Inc.

Company Background

Solvay Polymers, Inc., (Solvay) is the wholly owned subsidiary of Solvay, S.A., the $9.2 billion Brussels-based global chemicals and pharmaceuticals giant. Roughly 10 percent of the parent company's revenues can be directly attributed to the business efforts of its American subsidiary. Solvay, S.A. acquired the company in 1974 from the Celanese Corporation to augment its plastics business. In 1990, the company's name was changed to Solvay Polymers, reflecting its close working relationship with the parent company.

Solvay is committed to developing and sustaining effective leadership. Each year, the company completes the Malcolm Baldrige National Quality Award[1] self-assessment. It is used as an indicator of how well the company is doing in achieving its goals of competitiveness, customer satisfaction, and continuous improvement. These three Cs, or long-term critical success factors (CSFs) as the company calls them (see figure 8.1), are directly tied to, and play a large role in, how leadership and leadership development is viewed and directed throughout the Solvay organization, including finance.

For example, under Vice President Finance Guy H. Mercier, the 40-person finance department has become integrated into the company's businesses. Today, finance's goal is to be viewed as a business partner, identifying risks and developing the requisite metrics (figure 8.1) to achieve each department's CSFs. To facilitate these objectives, finance executives at Solvay recognize that they need to acquire and maintain more than just the traditional hard skills of finance. They need to acquire the business competencies that will afford them the opportunity to be seated at the company's decision-making table and be seen as business partners.

Figure 8.1
Solvay's CSFs and Related Business Metrics

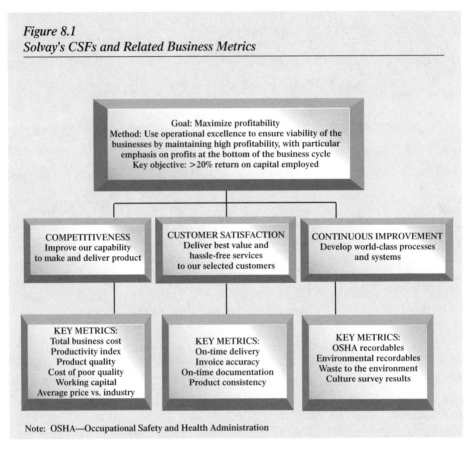

Goal: Maximize profitability
Method: Use operational excellence to ensure viability of the businesses by maintaining high profitability, with particular emphasis on profits at the bottom of the business cycle
Key objective: >20% return on capital employed

COMPETITIVENESS
Improve our capability to make and deliver product

CUSTOMER SATISFACTION
Deliver best value and hassle-free services to our selected customers

CONTINUOUS IMPROVEMENT
Develop world-class processes and systems

KEY METRICS:
Total business cost
Productivity index
Product quality
Cost of poor quality
Working capital
Average price vs. industry

KEY METRICS:
On-time delivery
Invoice accuracy
On-time documentation
Product consistency

KEY METRICS:
OSHA recordables
Environmental recordables
Waste to the environment
Culture survey results

Note: OSHA—Occupational Safety and Health Administration

This case is interesting for two reasons. First, many of the leadership competencies discussed throughout this book, such as communication, are purposely designed to be part of Solvay's organizational processes and business strategies. Thus, the company's leadership initiatives are focused on building a successful organization that capitalizes on the behaviors essential for teamwork and organizational learning. Second, the case presents some interesting views about leadership and leadership development from Guy Mercier, who brings to this study a multicultural perspective from both sides of the Atlantic.

Solvay's Leadership System

Setting Direction

Key to Solvay's ability to meet its critical success factors of competitiveness, customer satisfaction, and continuous improvement are how leaders set direction, communicate, participate in reviews, and improve the company's leadership system.

For example, one of the earliest improvement efforts initiated at the company was to break down functional barriers between all departments and individuals. This was accomplished by establishing an organizational (and cultural) framework of interfunctional teams and councils. They are responsible for directing and managing cross-functional aspects of Solvay's business, such as product and information technology strategies.

There are eight major teams or categories of councils. One of the most interesting is the CSF Council, of which there are three: One is responsible for competitiveness, another for customer satisfaction, and a third for continuous improvement. On each of these councils sit the senior leaders of the organization, including Mercier, as well as employees from all related business areas. The CSF councils have one fundamental purpose: They plan, manage, and direct company-wide improvement initiatives utilizing the Baldrige criteria as the benchmark for each CSF.

Another important council is the Management Council, which includes all the company's senior executives, among them David Birney, president of Solvay Polymers, and his six direct reports, one of whom is Mercier. In its Baldrige self-assessment, the company notes, "Overlapping membership by senior leaders and executives in other inter-functional councils ensures coordination and alignment. All planning and strategic direction issues are integrated into our inter-functional system."

Communicating and Reinforcing Values and Expectations

In its most recent Malcolm Baldrige self-assessment, the company highlights, "These inter-functional efforts have transformed our culture into one of high employee involvement and broad understanding of the issues that affect our business. The structure has also enhanced organizational learning through the inter-functional exchange of information and ideas." Thus, at Solvay the emphasis is on incorporating behaviors like good communication and information sharing into the company's organizational structure and business processes.

Moreover, Management Council members constantly reinforce the company's customer focus and expectations to all levels of the company through a series of ongoing activities. A sample of some of the most important of these leadership initiatives and responsibilities includes the following:

- Mentoring new employees

- Management by walking around

- Accompanying the sales force on numerous customer visits each year and hosting customer visits to the company's facilities

- Making presentations during training sessions

- Participating in the company's annual Malcolm Baldrige self-assessment

- Developing and leading training on quality- and business-related issues such as understanding financial statements, production and catalyst technology, and systems thinking and understanding the business cycle

- Contributing articles to the company's intranet and internal newsletter, *Quality Matters*

- Attending quarterly senior leaders' meetings where topics such as strategy and leadership are explored

- Taking an active role in presentations and discussions at the company's annual business meeting—which more than 30 percent of the company's employees attend each year on a rotating basis—and other routine employee meetings

The company notes,

These initiatives by Management Council members, in turn, drive additional communication and reinforcement efforts throughout the company by all managers and supervisors. In keeping with our emphasis on teamwork, senior leaders have sponsored and/or have been members of nearly 300 quality improvement teams since 1990. Sponsorship and/or membership has expanded the managers' role and has helped foster cooperation and better understanding among departments, in addition to driving improvement relative to our CSF objectives.

Evaluating and Improving the Leadership System

Solvay has implemented several approaches for reviewing the effectiveness of its leadership system. The company's Management Council champions these efforts, which include the following:

- Using deployment interviews. These interviews are conducted throughout the company to determine the extent of understanding of the company's mission and deployment of key approaches to achieve it.

- Conducting an annual cultural survey that includes questions relating to leadership effectiveness throughout the entire company.

- Implementing a 360-degree performance evaluation system that is used throughout the company and that includes all senior organizational leaders.

These and other initiatives seek to build leadership qualities directly into the fabric and culture of the organization, including its business processes and strategies. But even beyond these organizational initiatives, the company's leaders bring some interesting perspectives to the leadership development process. Given Solvay's close ties to its European parent company, these cross-cultural views are especially noteworthy.

An Overview of Leadership: The Importance of Culture

Who is a leader? What constitutes leadership? What are leadership skills? Can they be developed? If so, how so?

In attempting to answer these broader questions about leadership, this company's case study reminds us that it is important to address the elements of leadership, and leadership development, from a perspective of cultural differences.

For example, although he now lives and works in Houston, Texas, Guy Mercier spent the earlier part of his career as a consultant, entrepreneur, and financial executive for the parent company in Brussels, Belgium. His extensive international background brings a comparative perspective to many cultural dimensions about leadership and leadership development that might otherwise be forgotten, or too easily taken for granted.

Mercier first notes that the entire approach to global leadership thinking is in transformation. This transformation of views is likely to reshape the way business looks at leadership and leadership responsibilities well into the next millennium.

He observes, "In Europe, the individual man still counts the most. But here in the United States, it is the team that really matters." He goes on to note, "However, even on a team you can't forget the individual. The fact is that some people make more of a difference than others do. We no longer view such individuals as being kings or stars. Instead, we look at such people more like corporate heroes. Today, the key difference is that when a hero or leader is recognized as such, they must be able to make a difference—not by themselves or for themselves—but rather for the entire corporation, and most importantly, together with their team."

Another important area that Mercier discusses is the role of leaders in achieving organizational efficiency and effectiveness. Organizational efficiency is focused on quality improvements and process reengineering. Total quality management or just-in-time inventory management are good examples. On the other hand, organizational effectiveness is more oriented to growth, such as increased market and customer share. Both these goals frequently require difficult decisions to be made, and good leaders must make sure that valuable people, critical for achieving each goal, do not go unnoticed (or lost) in the process.

In this latter regard, Mercier observes, "Because of the American emphasis on getting things done, a good leader must build extra mechanisms to protect certain personalities. This is especially true for individuals who might be viewed more as thinkers than doers."

He goes on,

I am not suggesting that finance, or any department, should create intellectual islands or isolated laboratories. However, from the highest level, as a leader, you need to keep an eye on these more pensive individuals. They are a valuable resource that should be nurtured. In this respect, leaders must always be godfathering, which is more than mentoring. It is about listening and sharing. It is about truly caring about someone and his or her needs. It is about ensuring that the organization recognizes the importance of a wide diversity of talent and related contributions that add value to both the efficiency and longer-term growth objectives of the organization.

Financial Leadership: Identifying Key Competencies

According to Mercier, today there are two forces that influence the competencies required for financial leadership. One of these is external, and the other is more internal. The external factor is the speed at which today's international financial markets move. The internal factor is the growing expectation that financial executives will partner with their business counterparts. From these two forces, or pressure points as he calls them, the requisite leadership competencies for financial executives naturally flow.

In responding to our study's questionnaire protocol (see the appendix), Mercier discussed a wide range of competencies. After noting the more traditional importance of mathematical skills and accounting expertise, he put forth the following list of leadership competencies that he feels play a key role in the leadership development of a financial executive.

Risk Management

High on Mercier's list of competencies for financial executives is risk management. According to him, the risk manager is not necessarily the person who takes the risk—that is the business manager's role. Rather, the risk manager is the person who measures, controls, and eventually hedges the risk and has the ability to ask, and help ascertain answers to, such important questions as—

- What profit will be eliminated if the businesses take these risks?

- How can we retain that profit—build in a risk premium?

- What is the net added value produced with the company's capital?

- Did we reduce or increase the shareholder's risk to achieve that added value?

Usually the finance person is seen as the bad guy. "He or she is viewed as being risk averse," he says, adding, "This need not be the case, especially if the finance person is viewed more as a business partner. To accomplish this, the finance person needs to be able to communicate effectively, translating risk into business and organizational objectives."

Mercier believes that risk management is the one area of finance that should never be outsourced. In this sense, it is a true core competency of finance. Mercier explains it this way:

> Today you need permanent reengineering, both internally and externally. You need to be flexible and be ready to promote that. This even goes for accounting. But accounting is only figures and by outsourcing it you won't—as some seem to believe—lose your control. In contrast, however, the only finance activity you really can't afford to outsource is risk management. Risk management goes beyond the figures. It is more about the quality of the risk you are taking. It is about comparing and getting actual experience with the different risks themselves. It is impossible to outsource that knowledge or experience to others without seriously damaging the effectiveness (growth) of the whole business organization.

Stress Management

Another competency that is becoming more important for financial leadership development is stress management. He notes, "Working online is a major source of stress for financial executives today. Unlike the past, you don't have time to come back and prepare your figures and scenarios. Increasingly, we have to deliver online, real-time data while still maintaining accuracy and credibility as the guardian of the rules."

Besides the stress of technological challenges, there is recognition at Solvay of the stress that comes from today's fast-moving markets and the increasing pressure on financial executives to make a meaningful contribution to the business. In the past, finance was a very well-defined set of skills and tasks. Today, however, largely because of increased efficiency, many of these previously defined tasks have been outsourced or significantly reduced in terms of their internal importance.

That means financial executives increasingly need to redefine their work in terms of how they can add value to the businesses. Put another way, the emphasis on financial efficiency—for example, cost minimization, financial process reengineering, and outsourcing—is increasingly augmented by pressures on financial executives to contribute more value directly to the businesses themselves—for example, an understanding of enterprise-wide risk and related business solutions.

Given these pressures, financial executives are finding themselves under increasing stress. According to Mercier, "Financial executives who don't handle stress well become rigid and intolerant to change. They increasingly retreat into what they are comfortable with and what they know already works. They are simply not prepared for an ever-changing world and certainly are in no position to partner with the businesses of an organization."

Mercier is no stranger to the pressures of today's changing environment. At the time of this interview he had 148 prioritized items on his things-to-do list. When asked how he handled the pressures of his job, he offered the following reflections:

1. First and foremost, always try to keep a healthy balance between your family and work life. It is important to maintain the balance if you want someone to perform for you in your business. As is frequently said, "As the home front goes, so does the war."

2. Have a long-term view of what you do and why you are doing it. For example, some day Mercier would like to see his children work for Solvay.

3. Keep meetings to a predefined period each month. Mercier allocates one week per month for meetings. As he prepares his

business calendar, he always frees up that week for prioritized meetings, and then says no to the rest.

4. Make yourself accessible but not always immediately available. For example, ask colleagues to leave e-mail or voice-mail messages but don't build expectations that you will be available to speak with them when you are working in different time zones.

5. Have a good attitude about what you know and what you don't. In a technological environment, everyone can't know everything about everything. The market is changing too fast. Always just do the best you can.

6. Don't fall victim to the drug of stress. For example, if the company's return on capital targets have been met, don't be afraid to ask for a bit of the additional marginal cost to improve the team spirit.

7. Be ready to admit a mistake. The stress to work online is increased even more if you are afraid to make, or admit, an error.

Communication

The importance of communication is reinforced by Solvay's corporate culture and the communication mechanisms it has implemented to expedite communication.

For example, meetings are not seen as a negative at Solvay. In fact, one week per month is designated as the time when meetings are held to ensure that information is cascaded throughout the entire organization. As Mercier notes, "Cascading information is very important to the success of our business. Cascading is a very powerful communication process."

In addition to the fact that finance has a presence at all meetings during this week, Mercier notes the important role that finance has played in terms of developing a very powerful internal reporting system:

By the fifth day of the month we are closing and by the tenth day we have created operating statements and roughly 20 business metrics. These metrics are then boiled down to four key measures; namely, return on capital, total business cost, product consistency, and safety.

Variable compensation at the company is linked to these four measures. Also, after the tenth day of the month, finance sends out a one-page summary of all these figures, which is the same summary that is used to kick off day one of meeting week. However, when we get together for meeting week, we don't emphasize the figures. Everyone has seen these already. Instead we spend our time discussing their implications, the trends and the strategies for the business. The reality of our business is today and tomorrow—not the past.

Finally, Mercier notes the importance of the company's ten-year business model to the internal communication process. Developed by finance, under the auspices of President David Birney, the model is very dynamic. Mercier explains, "Everyone inputs into the model and it is shared with everyone. It is a very powerful business tool. The ten-year business model is also used to communicate our business progress to our parent company and to validate our five-year business plan."

Cooperation

Demonstrating cooperation, according to Mercier, is extremely important in changing the perception about finance from a control function to the role of a business partner and advocate. This shift required some important changes in internal thinking and behavior.

Mercier notes,

Today, the only real power you have as a finance person is to influence business decisions in the right directions, and to make available the financial resources business people need to accomplish their goals. To get that influence, you need to be viewed as a partner. You need to be at the business table with the freshest figures and benchmarking data. Also, it is important to remember who your partners really are. As a finance person, your true partners are the internal business people that you have the ability to create shareholder value with. With a partner, you are doing the job together, and that means cooperation is an extremely important competency for a financial executive to either possess or develop.

Consulting Skills and Customer Orientation

Next on Mercier's list are consulting skills and a customer orientation. He believes that consulting skills and a customer approach are two very important competencies for a financial executive to possess and should be discussed together.

For example, while he strongly believes that the partners of finance are internal operating people, when it comes to customers, he believes finance needs to be more all-encompassing. The customers of finance include shareholders, the executive committee, the president, the finance team, the business managers, and even the market. He explains,

> As a consultant, I have to understand the expectations of all these customers and integrate them into a meaningful financial strategy. The best way to do this is through a financial risk management approach, including the benchmarking of processes, costs, asset structure, customer satisfaction, return on capital employed in the business, etc. By having good consulting skills, rather than criticizing, finance is measuring and bringing a neutral comparative perspective to the business.

Mercier has four analysts who are devoted to providing metrics to the business. Concerning the organizational role that finance plays, he observes, "We are not a cost or separate profit center. We are partners and we just try to produce direct financial value-added. For example, one of our goals is to try to provide suggestions that will reduce cost—not just for finance but everywhere in the company—by 5 percent."

Other Competencies

While the above competencies rate high on Mercier's leadership development list, there are other competencies that he feels are especially worth nurturing.

- *Interpersonal understanding.* Includes shareholders, business managers, the team, and employees.

- *Influence.* Mercier notes that in influencing others you must try to remain neutral. "Rather than promoting something, you are just trying to get someone to look at the alternatives and what might be a better approach. Influence is very important, but I remain very cautious over the correct use and interpretation of this competency."

- *Assertiveness.*

- *Relationship building.* He explains, "Business managers don't have the time to lobby with bankers, investors, and shareholders. Building relationships in these areas is an important competency for finance to bring to the business table."

Financial Leadership: Developing the Requisite Competencies

Mercier has outlined a challenging set of competencies for financial executive leadership success. The next logical question to ask is how are these competencies developed and nurtured at Solvay? What developmental support mechanisms does the company have in place? What tools does it use to monitor and promote the most appropriate behaviors for leadership success? At Solvay, leadership development is a step-by-step approach.

First, leadership development starts by hiring the right people. At Solvay, business knowledge, experience, and the ability to work with others, especially those outside of finance, are extremely important considerations. Mercier explains, "In promoting finance people, we are first looking at an individual's business knowledge, then their understanding of our group structure, and finally the added value they can bring to the table because of their financial knowledge. We love the business knowledge and the experience and try to move people around the organization as much as possible."

Second, leadership development requires a focus and investment in every person, embodied in the individual development plan (IDP). For every job in the company, including all finance positions, there is a one-page job description. These job descriptions, or position profiles, are posted on the company's intranet. These profiles, in many respects, serve as an internal benchmark for each individual to aspire to and become the basis for each person's IDP.

The IDP is an important developmental tool. It focuses on career development (what progress the individual would like to make), the experiences needed, the training required, and the training proposed. The IDP includes an individual's career expectations and the challenges he or she is willing to take on; namely, new experiences. Every person in the organization, including the president, has an IDP.

Competency tests are used mostly for technical matters; however, as part of the input for the IDP, individuals also receive feedback on their softer skills, such as communication, through 360-degree feedback. This feedback, coupled with skill-competency testing, focuses an individual's IDP for the next 12 months. According to Mercier, "Specifically, one can't move on to greater challenges at the company until he or she improves in these areas."

IDPs also relate to CSFs. It is interesting to note that not only does the corporation have a set of CSFs—for example, a 20 percent return on capital at the top of the business cycle and no less than a 10 percent return at the bottom—but so do departments and individuals. Competitiveness, continuous improvement, and customer satisfaction (the three Cs) influence everyone in the organization and are reflected in the specific developmental goals for each individual's IDP. For example, as noted earlier, one of finance's goals is to try to reduce costs everywhere in the corporation by 5 percent; each finance person's IDP reflects this expectation.

Third, leadership development is an ongoing process requiring extensive feedback and support mechanisms. In this regard, the company uses two primary mechanisms: 360-degree feedback and mentoring. Says Mercier, "When linked to the IDPs, 360s are really very powerful as a developmental tool." Twelve people, including business leaders and his direct reports, review him using a 360-degree feedback tool. These 360s are conducted once a year and are followed up by a midyear review with his boss, David Birney.

There is also an extensive mentoring program at the company. Every employee has a designated mentor. At Solvay, a mentor is not an individual's boss, nor does a mentor have to be from the same department. Rather, a mentor is someone who has gone through the company's mentoring program and is someone from whom an individual can freely seek advice and direction. It would not be unusual for a finance person's mentor to be a business manager in a nonfinance area.

Moreover, mentors are there only to give guidance. Employees in finance, for example, are not required to share their IDP or 360s with their mentor.

Finally, leadership development requires an emphasis on both performance and behavior; namely, identifying the requisite competencies for achieving desired performance. All of the above competencies are designed to influence an employee's performance and behavior. Like other companies in this research, before Solvay began emphasizing competency development, it focused on desired performance instead of expected behavior. This has changed. Today, competency identification and development are a key leadership priority for everyone at the company.

Mercier concludes, "We have integrated the performance metrics with the requisite behaviors, especially the softer skills like teamwork and communication. Now an individual's performance is being evaluated by the metrics—for example, the CSFs included in his or her IDP—while the behavior is being evaluated and monitored by the 360s and the mentoring process. It is finally a complete picture."

Endnote

1. The Malcolm Baldrige Quality Award, created in the United States by the National Quality Improvement Act (1987), seeks to promote excellence in organizations. Since its inception, more than 100,000 organizations have requested copies of the self-assessment criteria for internal purposes of improving competitiveness and performance excellence. It has become a benchmark for quality improvement for organizations around the world.

Synovus Financial Corp.

I believe these are among the most important investments this company will ever make. And I predict both of these—The Leadership Institute and Foundations of Leadership—will soon produce the greatest returns of any investments we have ever made.

James H. Blanchard, chairman and CEO

Company Background

S ynovus Financial Corp. (Synovus) is a diverse financial services company with more than $12.5 billion in assets and 10,000 team members across the southeastern United States, Canada, Mexico, and England. The company has experienced a period of rapid growth, with the number of Synovus team members more than tripling over the past decade. Synovus owns an 80.8 percent stake in Total System Services, Inc., one of the world's largest information technology processors. Synovus also includes Synovus Trust Company, Synovus Securities, Inc., Synovus Mortgage Corporation, and Synovus Insurance Services.[1]

In 1999, *Fortune* magazine selected Synovus as the "Best Company to Work for in America." Synovus was named 11th on the list in 1998, and in 2000 has been named number five. The reason for its ranking, Synovus maintains, is that it is an institution firmly grounded in traditional values. According to its 1998 annual report, "Every decision we make, every action we take, is based on our most fundamental ideals, the beliefs that built this company. Treat people right. Do what's right. Everyone should know someone cares."[2] These basic values and priorities have resulted in what has been called "a culture of the heart."

Such a culture places an absolute premium on people, relationships, leadership, and leadership development. Leadership development at Synovus is about teaching, facilitating, and living the company's values. A great deal of time, energy, and resources are spent translating these values into behaviors. Thus, leverage competencies, while not necessarily labeled as such, are highly valued, fostered, and developed. Further, Synovus is a competent organization. That is, not only does it actively develop skills among its leaders, it also practices competencies such as relationship building, communication, interpersonal understanding, and leveraging diversity on an organizational level. Leverage competencies are woven into the very fabric of the company.

This chapter is divided into three sections. The first provides an overview of Synovus' people development principles and initiatives as they relate to its corporate culture. The second reviews parts of the research interviews with some of the company's leaders. The final section outlines several of the processes Synovus uses to develop leaders.

People Development at Synovus: Overview

Synovus is a 112-year-old company that was founded and nurtured by religious, spiritual individuals striving toward high ideals. Long before the *Fortune* rankings, Synovus worked to be the employer of choice in any community it entered. Integral to this, and to its greater values, is its commitment to team member satisfaction, growth, and development.

Synovus experienced tremendous growth over the past decade. Its leadership made it a priority to ensure that its cultural values continue to find expression and were taught, nurtured, and expressed daily throughout the Synovus family of companies. This was even written into the corporate plan.

In 1996, People Development Exponent (PDE), or Personally Developing Everyone, was created for this purpose. Encompassing a variety of programs (some of which are discussed below), PDE is responsible for developing each individual at Synovus, and "attempts to capture our corporate soul."[3]

At the center of PDE and leadership development at Synovus are Leadership Expectations (figure 9.1). This is a leadership model that outlines four fundamental ideals: live the values, share the vision, make

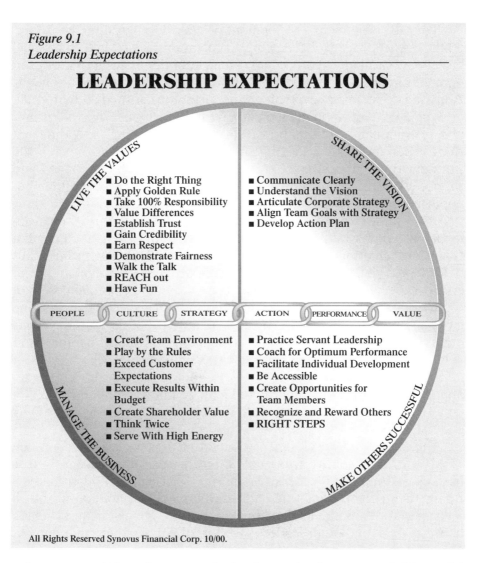

Figure 9.1
Leadership Expectations

LEADERSHIP EXPECTATIONS

LIVE THE VALUES
- Do the Right Thing
- Apply Golden Rule
- Take 100% Responsibility
- Value Differences
- Establish Trust
- Gain Credibility
- Earn Respect
- Demonstrate Fairness
- Walk the Talk
- REACH out
- Have Fun

SHARE THE VISION
- Communicate Clearly
- Understand the Vision
- Articulate Corporate Strategy
- Align Team Goals with Strategy
- Develop Action Plan

| PEOPLE | CULTURE | STRATEGY | ACTION | PERFORMANCE | VALUE |

MANAGE THE BUSINESS
- Create Team Environment
- Play by the Rules
- Exceed Customer Expectations
- Execute Results Within Budget
- Create Shareholder Value
- Think Twice
- Serve With High Energy

MAKE OTHERS SUCCESSFUL
- Practice Servant Leadership
- Coach for Optimum Performance
- Facilitate Individual Development
- Be Accessible
- Create Opportunities for Team Members
- Recognize and Reward Others
- RIGHT STEPS

others successful, and manage the business. At the center of this model is the Synovus value chain: people, culture, strategy, action, performance, and value. Leadership Expectations is ubiquitous at Synovus. It is a point of frequent discussion at all levels, and its components are continuously being refined and operationalized (defined in terms of concrete behaviors). The value chain gives each manager a people-based model for decision making.

Synovus' leadership development programs, either directly or indirectly, connect back to Leadership Expectations, which in turn connect back to the company's core values. Much attention is given to the development of skills that support the expectations and their components. A myriad of personal development opportunities, formal and informal, are available to develop team members. They include formal programs, classes, seminars, presentations, coaching, mentoring, and different work experiences. Undertaking projects both inside and outside the work environment is stressed. Community service is highly valued and supported, both as consistent with corporate values and as development opportunities.

Open and frequent communication, in a safe, supportive environment, is emphasized at the highest levels of the company. Jim Blanchard, chairman and CEO, holds weekly meetings with hundreds of leaders at all levels, continually reinforcing company values and leadership expectations. The Cultural Trust Committee is composed of representatives from every level and every company who meet with the CEO monthly to discuss the health of the corporate culture. Many other meetings among a variety of leaders and team members are held in which corporate values and expectations are reviewed and reinforced. Leaders are expected to be good listeners and create an atmosphere of trust and security to facilitate open communication, not only to discuss living the corporate values, but also to foster creativity and risk taking.

The leadership development of internal finance executives is the same as for all other Synovus leaders. Finance executives are viewed as business partners and leaders who are no different from other leaders. Again, their personal and leadership development is paramount, and all leaders share the same leadership expectations. No distinction is made between them and other leaders save for, of course, their unique technical abilities.

Leadership Perspectives on Cultural Values and Leadership Development

Elizabeth R. (Lee Lee) James, Vice Chairman, Synovus Financial Corp.

Lee Lee James,[4] as the chief people officer of Synovus, is one of its most valued leaders. She noted that Synovus has had the same HR strategy for 112 years. She emphasizes that it is an organization truly based on the golden rule. James described how the company's values and leadership expectations were written down, and structures and processes created, to ensure that Synovus remained faithful to its values.

She states, "At the same time, we wanted to make sure that everybody in the organization knew somebody cared about them. We did not want to be a big bureaucratic organization.... How you perceive your organization as a team member is directly related to how you feel about your supervisor. We have got to make it so that every supervisor is the best they can be."

James notes that Synovus' "culture of the heart" starts with role models at the very top of the organization and involves elevating the soft stuff:

We are different and we know we are. We do lift the soft stuff up a lot. We talk about love in our organization. Yes, believe it or not.... Our most senior leaders are inspirational.... They are not afraid to be emotional and feel it is okay to talk about love and that makes a difference.... If we had a leader who was cold and [only] bottom-line focused, we would have a very different organization.

In discussing the bottom line, James added,

We are [certainly] about creating shareholder value. We are also about creating wonderful customer service and taking care of our team. We work for something higher, and that's about doing the right thing for a lot of people.... While this impacts positively on our bottom line, it is not simply a means to an end. It is the right way to do business.

James reports that 2,000 leaders, including the CEO, will be participating in some form of leadership development program. She notes that "Our goal is to have a leader-full organization. We are not about hierarchy. We are team-oriented; anyone can have the next great idea. We want to foster that."

One of the processes developed to assist personal and leadership development involved the transformation of a performance evaluation process into a performance development process. Leverage competencies are routinely discussed in this Right Steps process. James related a story of how she spoke to an associate from another company who wanted to learn about some of Synovus' people development processes. On hearing about Right Steps, the person said that his company did something like this, but called it a competency evaluation performance assessment. His company, however, had difficulty implementing the program because of a lack of acceptance among team members, who found it threatening.

At Synovus, competency development is embedded in the context of a people-focused, relationship-rich, supportive culture. James reports that, in such an environment, most team members tend to feel secure enough to say "this is what I know I need to work on," whether it's technical skills or leverage competencies. The concept of "take 100 percent responsibility" at Synovus fosters, if not demands, such an attitude.

William Nigh, Senior Vice President, Synovus Financial Corp.

Bill Nigh also takes his role as leader and mentor very seriously. Inspired by Jim Blanchard, Nigh began to study leadership and leadership development in earnest about five or six years ago. He emphasizes that leadership development cannot just be "an event":

> While important, [formal leadership] training courses are events. I go, and I'm charged up, and it might change me for a week. In two weeks, I've got 50 percent of it, and in three weeks nobody ever knew I went.

Thus, according to Nigh, competency development must be an ongoing process. Under the concept of "take 100 percent responsibility," manager and team member are both held accountable for this process. Nigh states, "I have to make [competency development] happen. I have to help people change." To encourage his team to do this, Nigh began monthly leadership meetings. The role of discussion leader rotates among group members, and books on leadership are studied and discussed. Nigh notes that it is a point of great satisfaction for him that people at these meetings have given him constructive criticism: "I know the natural aversion that people have to being honest with the boss. Being able to give me grief in the context of leadership discussions is wonderful."

Giving the boss and coworkers "grief" must take place in an atmosphere of trust and support, which Nigh makes every effort to create. This begins and ends with relationships, especially the relationship between managers and team members. He mentioned a finance executive on his team with whom he is working to develop leadership skills. The executive expressed a lack of confidence to improve. Nigh told the person "Don't worry, I love you. We'll make it work."

The use of the word "love," mentioned earlier, must be understood in the context of the cultural value of unconditional love, discussed at the highest levels of the organization. Nigh adds that this does not mean, however, that team members are not held accountable for their own professional development and superior job performance.

He reports that the executive will enter one of Synovus' formal leadership development programs soon, adding:

> It will help, but this person must have me as a support system to come back to and have it not be an event. I take responsibility to make that happen. Assessment at the training program may be especially helpful for this team member. It can open this person's eyes tremendously. Leadership development is my role, my responsibility.

Stephanie Alford, EVP, People
Synovus Financial Corp.

Stephanie Alford is responsible for designing and implementing Synovus' leadership development programs. The company has devoted a great deal of time, energy, and resources to create programs and structures for leadership training. Alford reports that $2 million per year has been spent on this, all the more impressive given that Synovus has recently spent a great deal of money on new technologies. She points out,

> Our number-one assets are the people on our team. We can't afford not to invest in leadership development.... Bill Turner, our former chairman and CEO (and grandson of the founder of Synovus) had the philosophy that if we take care of our people, our people will take care of the customers and the profits will take care of themselves.

Again, however, while taking care of your people contributes to the bottom line, Alford emphasizes that people development and Synovus' people-oriented values are not simply a means to this end:

> If performance is our motive, then we won't get it right.... It's not necessarily a wrong motive to have. It certainly is not a wrong output to desire.... Certainly we're in the business of making a profit. We're results oriented. But if the fostering of these values in our culture is simply [a means to an end], we'll lose our culture.

Alford discusses, in this context, how the value chain, described earlier, assists in keeping business decisions tied to the company's values. When making a business decision, a series of questions is asked with regard to this chain, which starts with people and moves through culture, strategy, action, performance, and value: "How does the decision affect our people, whether they are team members, customers, or shareholders? Does it fit within our culture? What strategy will be the strategy used to make that decision? What strategies does it support or diminish? What actions will be used to implement that decision? What performance is expected? And, ultimately, what kind of value will it create?"

At Synovus, leadership development does not start in the classroom. It begins with the hiring process, in which team members get to know the candidate and his or her values, and the candidate does the same. It continues in the orientation program, which, states Alford, is "Sheer culture, a culture that is very rich and very deep. From day one, the message is given that you will be successful in getting your work done only if you know our values—know them, embrace them, and practice them." Alford adds that because "Synovus truly operates in a family-like atmosphere, there is a great deal of relationship building that happens before someone ever enters a classroom."

According to Alford, "The soft stuff and competencies have always been important at Synovus because people and relationships have been important." She, like Nigh, notes the importance of the company's investment in all the leadership development programs and state-of-the-art courses, yet observes that much of it comes down to relationships, especially the relationship between individuals and their managers:

> We offer the full range of [competency] development—executive coaching, training courses, mentoring, experiential development opportunities, and so forth. But in terms of engaging people on an individual basis throughout our organization, it's really between the individual and his or her manager. We truly believe that if we allow opportunities for that relationship to be strengthened, then everyone will have customized opportunities to grow and develop.

Relationship building is an important element in dealing with the diversity issues that have arisen with Synovus' rapid expansion. Relevant here is the leadership expectation of "live the values," with an emphasis on such components as valuing differences, building trust, and demonstrating fairness. Concludes Alford, "We have challenges with this, but everybody has a heart, and if we can figure out how to engage that heart, we'll be there.... We have folks in Canada, Mexico, and London. And our clients come from all over the world. We have to figure out how to engage people no matter where they're from."

Servant Leadership

Walter (Sonny) Deriso, Jr., Vice Chairman of the Board, Synovus Financial Corp.

Sonny Deriso is an example of a leader at the most senior level of Synovus who embraces and lives the company's values. Deriso emphasizes the notion of servant leadership at Synovus:

> If you're a servant leader, you're a leader who sees your responsibility as meeting the highest needs of the people you lead. It's

about not seeking the greatest role, but seeking the least role. In doing so, you're going to meet the needs of the people you serve.

Deriso approaches diversity issues in much the same way as Alford. He states that the company has had to learn that "the world doesn't necessarily operate [like us], and there are many things we learned from being exposed to other cultures—probably more than they learned from us."

He reported that Total System Services Inc., an affiliate of Synovus, expects to be in China in the future. In discussing Synovus' spiritual values, based on the Judeo-Christian tradition, with respect to working in China, he emphasized finding common ground in universal values. He relates a Chinese proverb: "If you want a year of prosperity, grow grain. If you want ten years of prosperity, grow trees. If you want a hundred years of prosperity, grow people." Says Deriso, "That's the philosophy that we try to live here.... Of course there are differences. But if you recognize and respect some basic values that are universal, we will be successful in adapting [to diverse cultures]."

He also addressed the need to remain humble and keep the right perspective in the face of the recognition from *Fortune*:

> We recognize that we are probably not actually the best place to work in the country. We want to be, and we may be, one of the best places. But the bar's been lifted and now if there's an area within our company that isn't a "best place to work," people are speaking up and saying, "We need to address something here because we're not living the way we are supposed to." So it has helped us become a better company by simply receiving the recognition.

Finally, the vice chairman points to a new challenge for Synovus:

> While our performance has never been better, we have never faced the period of uncertainty that we're facing right now. Companies that aren't yet in existence are going to be selling products that haven't been developed over channels that haven't been engineered—next week, and the week after that. Our challenge, in such an environment, is to maintain the human quality in what we do, keep the emphasis on people. If we do that, we'll be successful. And we will.

Leadership/Competency Development Processes at Synovus

The following are descriptions of Synovus' major development processes. At the time of the interviews, Synovus was in the process of combining all its efforts into the Center for People Development.

In-House Corporate Training

Synovus offers hundreds of training opportunities and courses on everything from commercial lending to BabyTalk, a class for new parents. Effective Presentation Skills, Effective Meeting Skills, Basic Stress Management, Effective Communication Skills, and Power Coaching are just some of the courses available to develop leverage competencies.

Team members may be offered external courses or training if they are not available at Synovus. The company prefers to train in-house, so courses can be tailored directly to the needs and values of Synovus' team members and facilitate networking and team building.

Foundations of Leadership (Foundations)

Foundations is required for all managers and supervisors. It is a four-day program over four months, focusing on teaching leaders the Synovus leadership expectations and how to demonstrate those skills in the workplace. Each day is devoted to one of the four leadership expectation quadrants. Every expectation and its components is broken down into specific behaviors. The program incorporates formal classroom instruction, interactive learning exercises, and exposure to other leaders within the company. Staff members from the Center for People Development write the curriculum with people from line operations, and it is piloted/tested on different groups. Train-the-trainer courses are provided for facilitators.

The Leadership Institute at Synovus (The Leadership Institute)

The Leadership Institute provides intensive leadership training through three progressively advanced leadership programs. Programs range from one to two years and include individual assessments, personal development planning, classroom instruction, business simulations, and community-based and on-the-job learning projects designed to help leaders integrate new behaviors and skills in the workplace.[5]

The three programs are the Emerging Leader, Executive Leader, and Organizational Leader programs. The Emerging Leader Program includes team members with at least two years of experience with a Synovus company who are expected to reach positions of increased responsibility and leadership in the near future. The program is one year long and includes two one-week sessions. The Executive Leader Program is offered to senior leaders responsible for divisions, business units, or certain strategic projects. It is 18 months long and includes three one-week sessions. The Organizational Leader Program is available to top-level executives, including presidents and CEOs. It is two years long and includes four one-week sessions.

Each program builds on the others. That is, the Executive leaders have already participated in the first two weeks of training, and the Organizational leaders in the first three. The programs are not limited to the off-site, one-week sessions. For example, emerging leaders are required to conduct either a work-related or community-based project under the supervision of more advanced leaders.

Figure 9.2 is an outline of the Emerging Leader Program. Note the integration of cultural values, leadership skills, and global perspective throughout the program.

Assessment and personal development planning are key features of the Leadership Institute. The first week of the program is based on developing self-awareness. Participants receive a battery of tests and measurements in addition to a number of 360-degree feedback evaluations focused on various competencies such as trust and ability to learn.

At the end of the week, participants meet with a psychologist for half a day to receive feedback and begin work on a personal development plan. Details around the results of the assessment are confidential, although participants are encouraged to integrate part or all of the development plan into their Right Steps (see below) discussions with their manager.

In keeping with Synovus' emphasis on balance and family, spouses are invited to participate in the first part of the program. In fact, the spouse participates in some of the assessment activities, and some of the feedback and development planning may even relate to personal and family issues.

Figure 9.2
Emerging Leader Program

The Leadership Institute at Synovus Emerging Leader Program is an instructional course designed to equip emerging leaders with the tools they need to assume greater levels of organizational responsibility. The program requires a one-year commitment and includes two one-week, off-site sessions.

LEADING-EDGE INSTRUCTION FEATURES:

- Activity-based learning
- Business-driven project work
- Business simulations
- Classroom instruction
- Individual feedback
- Personal developmental planning
- Presentation opportunities
- Self-assessment

PARTICIPANTS WILL:

- Create specific personal developmental goals through self-assessment and individual feedback
- Develop skills in strategic decision-making and conflict resolution
- Develop a deeper appreciation for Synovus' cultural values
- Explore the international, political, and economic forces affecting business today
- Gain more global insight of the total organization
- Learn to value and manage differences in maximizing team success
- Learn ways positive leadership impacts customer satisfaction
- Understand how personal leadership style affects achievement of business objectives

WHO IS ELIGIBLE?

Experienced managers and supervisors recognized for outstanding performance and an ability to foster followership among team members. These participants will likely be obtaining positions of increased responsibility and leadership in the near future. Interested team members must have at least two years of employment with a Synovus company to apply. Participants are invited to attend after receiving senior management recommendation, completing an application, and interviewing with a panel and external leaders.

Figure 9.2
Leadership Expectations (Continued)

ABOUT THE LEADERSHIP INSTITUTE

The Leadership Institute at Synovus is a key component in a series of initiatives designed to encourage growth and personal development while preparing Synovus team members to become front-runners into the 21st century. Fostering synergy through the "reach one, teach one" principle, The Leadership Institute at Synovus empowers individuals to encourage development in others, each one gaining strength through higher levels of personal growth and achievement. Its mission is to develop leaders who embrace, practice and impart the values of the Synovus family of companies.

As evidenced by CEO Blanchard's quote that begins this chapter, Foundations and the Leadership Institute enjoy tremendous support from the top of the organization. It is believed that these programs are playing a critical role in positioning the company for continued success in the financial services industry well into the future.

Right Steps

Right Steps is a continuous performance development planning process. It is a shift in emphasis from evaluation and judgment toward coaching and development.[6] Synovus ties the Right Steps process to the Make Others Successful area of Leadership Expectations. Figure 9.3 outlines the principles for building Right Steps.

Right Steps is a continuous cycle of these steps:

Step 1. Performance and development planning
Step 2. Periodic updates
Step 3. Year-end performance summary

Performance and Development Planning

Performance planning involves identifying three to five performance expectations that the manager and team member agree should be accomplished over a designated period, usually a year. Specific measures that will be used to monitor progress are identified. They can include

Figure 9.3
Our Principles for Building Right Steps

We used the following principles as a basis for RIGHT STEPS.

- We are committed to growing and developing each team member.

- It is critical for us to align individual goals and expectations with department goals and expectations.

- Everyone will receive a written Performance Development Plan. Supervisors and team members need to update these plans annually and support performance plan expectations as well as personal development needs.

- A candid, annual discussion of career interests is a minimum expectation with at least one update meeting and a year-end summary meeting (minimum of *three* meetings annually).

- Managers and supervisors will provide frequent and honest feedback.

- Everyone will receive an annual written Year-end Performance Summary—with documentation completed and filed in a team member's personnel file.

- Both job-related results and behaviors will be a part of the performance assessment.

- The Year-end Performance Summary will not include ratings.

- Implementation of the RIGHT STEPS is the shared responsibility of the team member and his or her supervisor. Both should perform their respective roles well to achieve successful results.

any number of indicators, such as quantity, timeliness, or quality, depending on the work area.

The Right Steps Handbook notes that "core competencies" should be identified. The team member needs to master these competencies to achieve performance expectations. They are then incorporated into a development plan, which focuses on the development of leverage competencies. Regarding this aspect of Right Steps, the handbook states, "Personal development is an integral part of Right Steps. It is not simply attending a few training programs or an occasional new assignment. A supervisor must incorporate team member development into every job he or she performs. Development must be a way of conducting business and not an afterthought."[7]

Development goals can include improving competencies related to short-term performance goals and to long-term career goals, such as moving to a higher level of responsibility. At least one major skill or competency to be developed is identified per year. Again, specific measures that will be used to monitor progress are established. For example, a certain number of activities involving public speaking might be established as part of a goal of strengthening this skill. (This, of course could be both a measure of progress and a development activity.) As discussed earlier, the manager and team member can select any number of training opportunities for professional development. Ongoing supervised developmental experiences, combined with ongoing coaching and support from one's manager, have been noted to be especially effective.

The Right Steps Handbook provides a checklist of skills and competencies to assist in the development planning process. See figure 9.4 for a sample of some of these competencies. Also, a skills application toolkit is available that focuses on ten leadership skills or competencies (e.g., developing team members, effective verbal communication skills, coaching skills).[8] The toolkit breaks the competencies down into specific behaviors and provides exercises and ideas for developing them.

Periodic Updates
A minimum of one midyear update is mandatory. It involves discussing progress made toward goals and modifications to goals, plans, or expectations. At least one documented meeting is required and more are encouraged. Further, ongoing communication and informal updates between supervisors and team members are expected, as is coaching provided by the manager. Of course, with the concept of taking 100 percent responsibility, both the supervisor and the team member take full ownership for their part in reaching the team member's developmental goals.

Year-End Performance Summary
At this meeting, the supervisor and team member review the progress made on the performance and development expectations, and discuss further performance and development planning. The supervisor acts more as a coach, discussing the team member's strengths and areas of opportunity, assisting the team member in aligning professional goals with organizational goals and expectations, and helping the team member explore ideas and options for improving future performance.

Figure 9.4
Skill Development Planning Checklist (A Sample)

Skill: Improving Processes
Knows and understands the basic quality philosophy of the company
Identifies and solves quality problems
Makes sure all improvements satisfy a customer's needs
Measures and records the results of quality improvements
Makes quality an integral part of the work process
Makes continuous improvement an integral part of a personal work philosophy

Skill: Managing Stress
Identifies and monitors potential workplace stressors
Works to eliminate workplace stress
Recognizes signs and symptoms of personal stress
Proactively manages personal stress
Understands options available to help reduce stress, including company sponsored options
Communicates stress-related problems, issues and solutions to management on a regular basis

Skill: Meeting Effectively
Contributes ideas, opinions and feelings during the meeting
Volunteers for action responsibilities during the meeting
Follows up effectively on all assigned responsibilities after the meeting
Offers constructive suggestions to improve meeting efficiency

Skill: Participating in the Corporate Culture
Knows and understands the corporate history and specific corporate culture
Models the components of the corporate image—professionalism and business etiquette
Understands and practices the principles of our Value Chain

Skill: Developing Self and Others
Defines goals and expectations for individual development
Uses the tools available within the company to grow and develop
Actively participates in creating a development plan with the supervisor
Follows through on developmental assignments

Conclusions

As noted at the outset of this chapter, Synovus is a competent organization. It may also be thought of as a functional family, one firmly grounded in spiritual values. It is a place that practices and promotes competencies such as communication, relationship building, interpersonal understanding, and team commitment.

The soft stuff is paramount at Synovus. The company has endeavored, however, to make it concrete by writing down its values and leadership expectations, defining the components and behaviors that make up and support those values and expectations, and making it a priority for every leader of the company to practice, teach, and facilitate those behaviors among team members. In addition, all business decisions are made using Synovus' value chain, which is an integral part of the Leadership Expectations.

Further, the company has invested aggressively in formal processes that help in making the soft stuff hard. It offers classes on a variety of leverage competencies. All managers and supervisors participate in Foundations of Leadership, a four-month program that teaches them the ins and outs of Leadership Expectations. The Leadership Institute offers more advanced leadership training for leaders, who range from up and coming executives to presidents and CEOs. Action-based training is emphasized, with leaders initiating community service projects in addition to on-the-job projects designed to develop leadership ability.

Right Steps has changed a performance evaluation process into a process of continuous performance development. Specific competencies are targeted for growth and development in this process. Most at Synovus would agree that, ideally, Right Steps should not be necessary. Right Steps involves communication and coaching between supervisors and team members. Leaders at Synovus work toward practicing communication and coaching daily, keeping in mind the notion of servant leadership.

Synovus develops its finance leaders the same way it develops its other leaders. This is a company that is not afraid to talk about spiritual values and unconditional love, let alone the soft stuff. Although most do not routinely use the language of leverage competencies at Synovus, anyone brought up right in this family, including financial executives, will practice them.

Endnotes

1. Additional information on this company can be found on the Web at www.synovus.com.

2. Synovus Financial Corp., *Annual Report,* 1998, 16.

3. Best Co. *The Synovus Guide to America's Best Workplace,* 24. (Columbus, GA: Synovus Financial Corp., 1998).

4. Mrs. James was promoted from president to vice chairman in May 2000.

5. Best Co. Ibid., 39.

6. *The Right Steps Handbook* (Columbus, GA: Synovus Financial Corp., 1998), 9.

7. Ibid., 26.

8. *On-the-Job Skills Application Toolkit* (Columbus, GA: Synovus Financial Corp.).

Unilever-HPC

Company Background

Unilever Home and Personal Care—USA (Unilever-HPC) is a $50 billion multinational consumer products company with over 300,000 employees across 90 countries. It produces a variety of food and home and personal care products.[1] In 1997, three Unilever companies in the United States, Chesebrough-Ponds, Lever Brothers, and Helene Curtis, integrated to form Unilever-HPC.

The interviews for this case study were conducted at Unilever-HPC—USA. Those interviewed included James Conti, HR director for finance; Paul Garwood, president and COO of the Laundry Business Unit; Greg Polcer, vice president finance, Unilever-HPC—USA; and Mark Landry, senior vice president, finance, Unilever-HPC—USA and North America. These senior executives offered their views and insights on the place of finance in their organization, and how leverage competencies and competency development may relate to that role. The first part of the chapter reviews these interviews.

Competencies have become central to the people processes at Unilever-HPC. Specifically, selection, performance assessment, development, and promotion processes are all based on competencies. The second part of the chapter outlines the Unilever-HPC global competency model and competency-based processes. Some of the processes discussed focus on those in Unilever-HPC. Most, however, are relevant to the entire global organization.

Financial Leadership at Unilever-HPC

The HR Perspective

James Conti sums up finance's ideal role at Unilever-HPC by stating that "We want to be the partner of choice.... Absolutely a strategic business partner.... To do that, we want to bring to the party not only our functional expertise, but beyond that a significant degree of leadership—leading the organization through financial understanding.... Helping our business partners understand what our financial health is and what opportunities that may present."

Conti maintains that there are a core group of competencies for finance that have everything to do with partnership:

> The ticket to the game is leadership skills, competencies such as the ability to develop others, team commitment, and leading others. Additional competencies take you to a higher level. These include influencing others, market orientation, and self-confident integrity.... A finance leader in the organization deals with key process holders with $40 or $50 million budgets. You're helping to manage that budget. Through analysis, you are involved in leading and guiding the organization through analysis and process skills. You have to have the market orientation to understand what's going on out in the marketplace, the influencing skills to sell [your views], and the integrity to stand your ground.

Conti outlined a number of processes designed to evaluate and develop competencies, not only for finance associates, but for all company employees. The details of these are discussed below. While these processes integrate competency development into the fabric of the organization through formal mechanisms, Conti noted that a challenge for the organization is to truly make competency development a part of the corporate culture: "How do we institutionalize these behaviors? How do we make them known in such a way that people say 'I need these things to be a leader. How do I put them into everyday practice? How do I develop them?' We continue to work on this."

The Business Partner's Perspective

Paul Garwood is a British national who has been with Unilever his entire career. He has had a varied career, including tenures across Europe, Asia, and the United States. As a leader of one of the company's largest businesses, he has been responsible for formulating its world-scale strategy. While with Lever Brothers, he was involved in a process designed to articulate that company's view of the finance function's role.

On this subject, Garwood's opinion is clear. He strongly believes in finance as business partner. He believes that the marketplace is changing "at a rate you natives don't actually recognize; it takes a visitor to notice some of these changes. Particularly in the context of dynamic revolutionary socioeconomic change, which is going to turn business on its head, I believe that having a business partner who approaches business issues from a financial perspective is an indispensable part of our multifunctional group designed to capitalize on those changes." Garwood comments further, "Just as there are some qualities that often appear in engineers—something to do with training or perhaps even genetic makeup—it's the person with the finance background who can provide a greater element of context and continuity to a subject or a discussion."

Regarding leverage competencies, Garwood believes there is an important competency that involves a curiosity about "what's going on out there":

> To occupy the position I'm talking about, which is a part of a multifunctional, multiprocess team, there is a competency which is about awareness of connections, interest in and curiosity about what's going on out there.... The breadth of perception one needs to operate effectively is getting broader. It's getting broader geographically and industrially, as boundaries start blurring and you suddenly find yourself in competition with somebody who you'd never have dreamt five years ago you'd be competing with.... "Curiosity" is linked to this greater breadth and to the ability to contribute to your team.

Garwood comments that soft skills are, ultimately, critical to being a successful business partner:

There is no room in this business for gurus who sit in offices [and] who need a staff of interpreters to manage the interface between them and the rest of the business. All of these things are a question of balance. There is no point in having the most insightful capabilities in terms of what's happening in the outside world if you can't articulate those inside the business in a fashion which is [at least] understood by, and [ideally] captures the imagination of others.

He noted that group and team-building skills are also important in this regard. Perhaps in part because of his wide experiences as an expatriate, he also emphasized the importance of leveraging diversity. He remarked, "There's no point in having diversity if you can't at least make 2 plus 2 equal 4.1. We've all seen occasions where it's added up to 3.9." Finally, Garwood astutely pointed out that leverage competencies interact with one another: "If I was smarter, I could map up multidimensional connections between all of these [competencies]."

Regarding competency development, Garwood believes that most leadership skills are the product of experience and can be developed, at least to some extent. As a result, he is very supportive of assessing competencies and creating personal development plans. He maintains that leadership abilities can be developed through work experiences designed for growth:

I'm a great believer in the idea that you start work on behaviors, and attitudes might, if you're lucky, follow. So you might take risks and assume someone can expand to fill the space. I have made mistakes, which is to put people in positions they proved to be incapable of doing. This is unfortunate because it can often take them backwards. I feel bad about that, but the alternative I feel even worse about. I don't claim to be infallible here, but if I'm 60 percent right I'm doing quite well.

The Finance Perspective

Greg Polcer is the functional equivalent of CFO for Unilever-HPC. Like Garwood and Conti, he falls squarely into the ranks of those who advocate for finance as strategic business partner. Yet all these executives stated that opinions vary across the company on the role that finance should play. Some believe in the more traditional conformance or command and control roles for finance, with much less emphasis on finance as business partner. Others clearly believe that finance is a strategic business function and a true player at the table. They all remarked that the three companies that integrated to form Unilever-HPC had very different cultures. As Polcer put it, "The three cultures were morning, afternoon, and evening." Thus, defining the role of finance at Unilever-HPC is a work in progress.

Polcer describes much of the role of the finance executive as that of consigliere, an internal consultant and confidante who partners with the most senior people in the organization. Such a partner "knows not only what's happening in the outside world, but the practicalities of what's happening on the inside." He also maintains that the senior finance person "is clearly the individual voice of conscience, one which represents the shareholder in an unbiased way.... To represent the shareholder at every table we go to." Another important role of the finance executive, in Polcer's view, is to assist in "strategy to action—how you actually take what we just said and make it happen in the real world." Polcer leads an operations committee that is involved in implementing the strategy set by the board of directors. He notes that leverage competencies play an important role here:

> The board sets the strategy, which we all agree to. We put that in an operational framework called the annual contract. As the year goes on, things don't always work out as designed. Now you get into interpersonal competencies. The people who I am dealing with have to have faith that I have more than just a bean counter's mentality, that I have a real sense of the business.... Influencing skills, relationship building, leadership, team commitment [and other competencies] are all relevant to building this credibility.

Polcer discussed the difficulty inherent in integrating three very different companies into Unilever-HPC. "It was a challenge working through the maze of 'if I say something to you it means something completely different to you than to me.'" He stated that finance provides a common denominator for the companies: "In the end, you have to report the numbers and how things are going in real dollars." As vice president finance, his job "was primarily a skill set about bringing people together." Sitting at the right hand of the COO, one of his roles was to help bring the cultures together and create a common language.

Again, however, Polcer noted that the finance function itself is still merging different cultures and approaches.

While Polcer emphasizes the role of finance executive as strategic business partner, he also stressed the importance of traditional finance skills:

> As you merge three companies with different processes and systems, the number one thing you have to do is maintain control. You maintain control through good financial skills, traditional skills. Until you do that you don't have the right to do anything else.

Polcer supports competency development for finance associates and was very familiar with the selection, evaluation, and development opportunities and processes the company provided. Like Garwood, he is a great believer in developing competencies through experience. He prudently suggests, however, that "Some things are hard to change. I'm not sure how far from the core you can change some people.... I've seen people with the desire to develop [certain competencies] but not the ability. This varies."

He, like Garwood, supports diversity and leveraging diversity, not just in terms of culture, race, and gender, but of different styles: "I've seen leaders who don't accept competencies which are exhibited differently from theirs. We need to respect different styles, to understand, for example, that someone may be as influential as me but do it differently."

Greg Polcer reports to Mark Landry, senior vice president Unilever-HPC and North America. Landry has been the COO of two Unilever companies: Chesebrough-Ponds USA and Lever Ponds-Canada. He notes that it is common at Unilever for CFOs to have been CEOs, and that many will become CEOs again. Such a background fosters a broad business perspective. Landry asserts that a finance executive should not only have a place at the business table, he or she should be sought after as "the talking partner of choice."

Landry shared some of his ideas and insights on the place of finance and the role of the CFO in an organization:

> The CEO sets the vision, which gets its expression and business context from close collaboration with the CFO. By its very nature the CFO role has a very neutral position in the business, and the CFO's traditional skills as well as training and business understanding, give

him or her a clear business perspective. It is incumbent upon the CFO to breath life into the vision.... If they are good, they will energize business...they will find new ways to actually encourage risk.

Corporate America has not distinguished itself by its vision. We must grow to sustain our premiums.... We'll have to grow through change. The role of the CFO will be huge here...in looking for innovation, change.... A finance person can create an environment which either shuts down ideas [or] gets people to take more chances.

I challenge [new managers]. When they bring a proposal to me, it has to be their proposal. They should never bring me a proposal and say this is what the team wants me to do and I have a problem with it. I ask them why they haven't been effective in getting their ideas through.... To assert based on your knowledge and passion for the business will always be welcome.

Landry understands the place of leverage competencies in such a partnership role. He is a strong supporter of learning and development. In fact, he sponsors the Finance Learning Network, which assesses the status of learning opportunities available for this function.

Regarding leverage competencies, like Polcer, Landry questions the extent to which some people can develop these skills: "Most things can be developed, but you have to have the foundation.... I believe that some qualities, such as courage and conviction, are either part of our makeup or not. If they are, the nurturing and the mentoring you get will make you a better leader." Added Landry, "One does not lead by exhortation, but by example."

As noted above, all of those interviewed emphasize the role of finance as strategic business partner. In addition, all acknowledged the relevance of leverage competencies in facilitating such a role, and supported its development. We will now provide an overview of the role of competencies at Unilever-HPC.

The Global Unilever Competency Model

In 1994, Unilever introduced a set of 11 competencies associated with superior performance among its managers.[2] The company identified these competencies by studying successful Unilever managers around the world to determine which characteristics and behaviors distinguished them from other managers in Unilever. (Unilever defines exactly what competencies are and are not in figure 10.1.)

Originally introduced as a tool to identify high-potential managers, the 11 competencies are now used globally to select new employees and to provide skill and career development for all manager-level employees.

For professional employees (supervisor and above), Unilever uses a level system to classify jobs (work level 2 = manager; work level 3 = director; work level 4 = vice president). Although the 11 competencies are the same across the work levels, the behaviors that compose the competencies are different across levels. Figure 10.2 describes a competency (entrepreneurial drive) at different work levels.

The 11 competencies are grouped under five clusters, each of which describes the qualities and actions of the effective Unilever manager.

The effective Unilever manager

- Possesses the intellectual power to determine direction

- Ensures that direction is market-driven

- Acts decisively to improve performance

- Delivers through people

- Achieves through integrity, teamwork, and learning

Figure 10.3 is a diagram of the Unilever Competency Model. It includes the five clusters with their supporting competencies.

A *Competency—Dictionary*[3] is available to employees. It provides the rationale for each of the 11 competencies, expanded behavioral descriptions at each work level, and behavioral examples for each competency. The *Competencies—Summary* notes that it is not possible to describe all the behaviors for each competency and that the examples are intended as a starting point rather than as a definitive list. This is

Figure 10.1
Competencies

ARE:

- Personal characteristics (self image, attitudes, values, traits, motives) shaping HOW a job is undertaken

- Factors contributing to superior job performance

- Measured through clearly observable behavior

ARE NOT:

- Knowledge and skills required to perform a job

- The tasks of a job

Unilever Home & Personal Care North America 1998

Figure 10.2
Competency Example: Entrepreneurial Drive

Acts decisively to improve performance

Someone who displays this competency:

Work Level

2	**Entrepreneurial Drive**
	- is highly motivated towards achievement and has a bias for action
	- actively seizes opportunities
3	**Entrepreneurial Drive**
	- constantly looks for new ways to improve business results
	- is persistent and resilient in overcoming obstacles
4	**Entrepreneurial Drive**
	- acts to create opportunities when others might take no action
	- takes initiatives often involving calculated risks
5	**Entrepreneurial Drive**
	- is restless in pursuit of major business improvements and successes
	- takes many actions over time to reach an entrepreneurial goal, changing direction and tactics to overcome obstacles

Each successive Level assumes competency at the lower Level(s).

Figure 10.3
The Unilever Competency Model

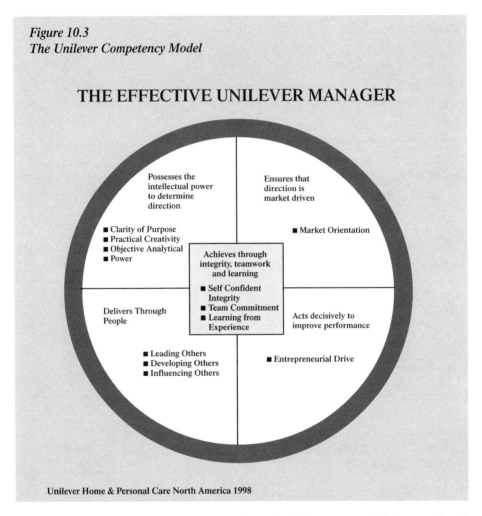

THE EFFECTIVE UNILEVER MANAGER

Possesses the intellectual power to determine direction

■ Clarity of Purpose
■ Practical Creativity
■ Objective Analytical
■ Power

Ensures that direction is market driven

■ Market Orientation

Achieves through integrity, teamwork and learning

■ Self Confident Integrity
■ Team Commitment
■ Learning from Experience

Delivers Through People

■ Leading Others
■ Developing Others
■ Influencing Others

Acts decisively to improve performance

■ Entrepreneurial Drive

Unilever Home & Personal Care North America 1998

especially important in terms of cultural differences, which may lead people to express competencies in different ways.[4]

Competencies at Unilever-HPC: Overview

Competencies are the foundation of people development systems at Unilever-HPC. Unilever-HPC's system for selecting new recruits (competency-based selection), both from universities as well as midcareer hires, uses key competencies determined to be critical for success on the job. After people are brought into the organization, they are assessed annually against competencies (and job skills), and a plan to develop competencies is created (performance development planning). Unilever-HPC offers a variety of learning opportunities for employees to improve their competencies.

In addition, HPC uses the Human Resources Planning Process (HRPP) to develop and manage the careers of its employees on a long-term basis. It is based on the extent to which employees demonstrate competencies (in addition to specific job skills) at the work level above the one they are currently in.

Competency-Based Selection

In 1998, Unilever-HPC implemented a competency-based selection system to identify people with the attributes and skills best suited for success at Unilever-HPC. In this process, candidates are asked questions that probe their competency level for several competencies that have been identified as critical to the job for which they are applying. Competency-based interviews are designed to collect accurate behavioral information about job candidates. This behavioral information is used to evaluate the candidate and ultimately to determine whether or not to make her or him an offer.

Interviews are constructed for specific positions by selecting a subset of the 11 competencies that represent the most important indicators of success on the job. Recently, finance hired a group of assistant commercial managers from MBA programs across the United States. Six competencies, including team commitment, influencing others, and practical creativity, were identified as key for this particular position. The choice of which competencies to use in an interview always involves the input of those with expertise in the job requirements. For example, an incumbent, or the person who would be managing the position in question, might, in partnership with HR, select the competencies to be included in the interview.

An interview protocol was then created for the assistant commercial manager position, which included questions designed to determine the candidate's skill level for each of the six competencies. Interviewers are given specific questions to ask for each competency and follow up with probing questions. Each question seeks specific, behavioral examples of a candidate's past job performance. These questions ask what the candidates would do in hypothetical situations or what they have done in the past. An example of a question that focuses on leading others is, "Recall an experience when you needed to convince a client, customer, or manager that their approach toward an issue was less effective than yours. What was the issue, and how did you persuade the other party to accept your viewpoint?"

Scoring standards (good answers versus poor answers) are determined in advance, and the interviewers use them to assess the candidate's responses to each question. For each competency, candidates are rated on a 1 to 4 (very strong to weak) scale. In many cases, panel interviews occur so that more than one person can rate a candidate's answers.

All employees who conduct interviews must be trained in the competency-based interviewing approach. This training is four hours long and covers how to construct the interview (identify the competencies and questions to include) for any specific job, how to prepare for and conduct the interview, and how to assess a candidate. Also, a significant amount of time is spent role-playing the interview process so that interviewers are comfortable with the approach when they actually conduct the interviews.

Performance Development Planning (PDP)

PDP is Unilever-HPC's performance assessment and development system, and is a fundamental business process that aims to foster individual growth and development. Unilever-HPC believes that motivated employees who are growing professionally will enable the company to meet its corporate growth objectives. Employees are required to achieve exceptional standards of performance, collaborate effectively with colleagues, embrace new ideas, and learn continuously.

PDP is more than just an annual review. It is about carefully planning performance and development, and it provides ongoing feedback about needed skills and competencies. PDP integrates the organization's goals, individual performance targets, performance assessment, development plans, and career discussions. It helps shape and influence employees' careers and helps them achieve challenging targets that they have agreed to pursue each year. PDP is seen as a joint responsibility between manager and employee; it is a tool that focuses on self-assessment, fueled by constructive feedback and guidance from managers.

The cornerstone of PDP is continuous dialogue about leadership growth. Noteworthy here is not only the emphasis placed on competency development, but also on placing it within the context of organizational goals.

The following are the three key elements of PDP:

Target Setting
Through the creation of SMART (stretch, measurable, achievable, relevant, and timeframed) goals, employees set performance targets and continuously monitor and evaluate their achievement. These targets enable employees to establish a clear direction for their work and challenge themselves to achieve stretch results.

Performance Assessment
PDP serves as the mechanism for open and honest discussions about overall performance through formal, annual reviews and follow-ups. These reviews focus on performance against specific targets, the quality of results, and relevant professional skills and competencies.

Development Planning
Development plans are centered around skills and competencies that the employee needs to develop. PDP also includes discussions about long-term career growth and development.

The PDP Process
The following are the eight steps in the PDP process:

Step 1: Understand the Business Objectives and Priorities. Each year, the CEO issues a *Business Objectives and Priorities* booklet. It provides employees with sufficient understanding about the direction of the business so they can set goals within the context of the business direction.

Step 2: Set Individual Performance Targets. Each employee develops performance goals from the *Overall Business Objectives and Priorities* and from his or her department's or team's goals.

Step 3: Define the Skill Requirements of Position and Assess Skills Against the Job Skills Profile. Job skills profiles for each position and a professional skills dictionary help the manager and employee to determine the critical skills required for the particular job and employee skill level.

Step 4: Assessment of the Unilever-HPC Competencies. Using a competency assessment form, each employee assesses himself or herself against the Unilever-HPC competencies. In addition, managers complete one form for each of their direct reports.

Step 5: Assessment of Performance Against Previous Year's Targets. Each employee completes a form that measures how well he or she performed against the goals set for the previous year. Managers complete this form for direct reports as well.

Step 6: Performance Assessment Meeting with Manager. The employee and manager meet to discuss the previous year's performance as well as the skill and competency assessments. Where feasible, performance and competency assessments include 360-degree feedback.

Step 7: Creation of Skill and Competency Development Plan. Following the performance assessment meeting with the manager, a development plan is constructed that takes into account the outcome of the skill and competency assessments and the goals and targets of the employee and his or her organization. Specific skills and competencies (usually one to three) are targeted for the coming year. The employee's manager agrees to the plan. HR may assist the employee and manager in finalizing the details of the development plan.

Step 8: Follow-up Career Development Meetings with Manager. The employee and manager meet to discuss the employee's progress on the development plan, as well as the employee's aspirations for career and future goals. Managers present the company's view on the employee's future potential, which is determined in the HRPP.

HRPP

For Unilever-PPC, HRPP is a focused effort that will help to ensure it has capable leaders for the future. The process includes the identification of employees with high potential, a discussion and review of individual development plans, and succession planning. It also involves a series of formal reviews or roll-up meetings, along with discussions between line managers and their HR counterparts to assess employee potential and discuss development and career options.

Employees are rated against job skills and competencies to see if they are performing at the level of their current job or of a higher-level job. If they are demonstrating competencies at the higher level, they are deemed high potential and are expected to reach the more senior level within the next three years.

HRPP and PDP

PDP is about performance and growth for individuals in their current roles and positions. HRPP, however, is about training individuals to assume leadership roles and positions for the organization in the future. The information from PDP (the competency assessment) and the individual's own career goals feed into the HRPP process and are used to help assess potential. Succession planning and nominations for specialized training that result from the HRPP, in turn, become input for follow-up PDP career discussions.

Again, competencies play a critical role in this process. They are one of three components of weighing an employee's potential. The other two are relevant experience and skills and performance:

> "High Potential" managers will display competencies and behaviors which are typically required at higher work levels. They will have acquired an appropriate breadth and depth of experience and skills to prepare them to undertake these substantially more challenging positions in the future. They must, of course, also have a strong track record of delivering consistently good performance.[5]

Competency Development

Unilever-HPC has a Web site called the Learning Resource Center that contains specific information about how to develop each competency. For example, an employee who needs to become a better leader might log onto the Leading Others section of the Web site to see different ways of learning this skill. Also, Unilever-HPC has networks across the company called the Learning Resource Network. For each business area or function, a group of employees identifies specific learning needs. As mentioned earlier, Mark Landry sponsored the Finance Learning Network, which is responsible for capturing key learning needs and opportunities for the finance function.

Unilever-HPC takes a very broad approach to competency development. In addition to training courses offered in the United States and through Unilever-HPC corporate's training office in London, Unilever-HPC recommends and regularly employs a broad array of personal development activities to enhance competencies. Figure 10.4 shows ongoing personal development activities offered throughout Unilever.

Figure 10.4
Ongoing Personal Development Activities

Job Rotation	Classroom Training	On-the-Job Training
Job Enrichment	Task Forces	Acting Assignments
Assignment Rotation	Instructor Training	Workshop Leader Training
Colleges	Universities	Community Service

Unilever Home & Personal Care North America 1998

These include the following:[6]

- *Job rotation.* Places individuals in different jobs or on other teams in the organization to develop skills.

- *Classroom training.* Attendance at classroom sessions to develop new knowledge and skills.

- *On-the-job training.* Time spent as an understudy on the job. The purpose is to learn as much as possible from someone who has demonstrated technical skill or knowledge of a topic or who is highly skilled in a specific competency.

- *Job enrichment.* Expands an individual's duties beyond the normal job description. Gives additional responsibilities to the person, but should not be used if the employee currently does not meet or exceed the standards and objectives of the job.

- *Task forces.* The employee serves with other employees in analyzing and developing business opportunities to get a chance to contribute to the business in a new way. Task forces also give individuals a chance to broaden their organizational knowledge and develop a network with others.

- *Acting assignments.* Employee becomes the acting replacement when someone is away from the job. Gives employees a chance to see how they handle added responsibilities.

- *Assignment rotation.* Rotates people through the same or similar jobs as a learning experience. Broadens a person's knowledge of the organization while building new skills.

- *Training instructor/workshop leader.* Develops effective employees by having them teach others the skills they have learned on the job.

- *Colleges and universities.* Attendance at local colleges and universities that have recognized the need to better serve working adults who want to improve themselves.

- *Community service.* Community service and volunteer work provide individuals with an excellent opportunity to grow personally and become better business leaders and citizens.

Figure 10.5 diagrams the use of competencies at Unilever-HPC, and is relevant to all of Unilever.

Summary

Unilever-HPC was formed through the integration of three Unilever companies with three different cultures. While acknowledging diverse opinions on finance's place in the organization, all the interviewees indicated substantial support for the role of financial executive as strategic business partner. They also recognized the importance of leverage competencies for finance executives and supported their development.

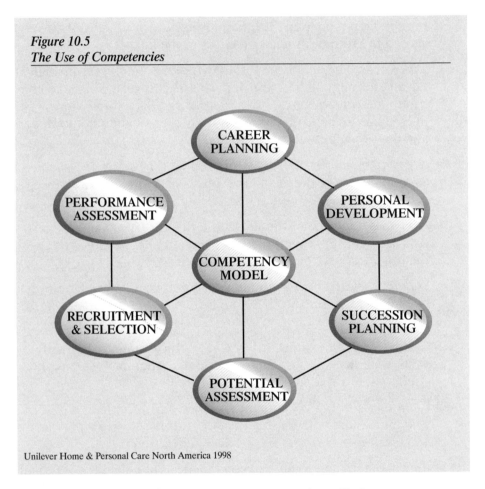

Figure 10.5
The Use of Competencies

Unilever Home & Personal Care North America 1998

Some believed, however, that there may be a limit to competency development. That is, some people will naturally be stronger in certain competencies than others, and some may have the desire to change but not the capacity. All agreed, however, that some competency development was possible and desirable. It was also noted that competencies may be expressed through a variety of styles and behaviors, and that diversity should be valued and encouraged.

Unilever-HPC developed a global competency model by examining the behaviors of successful leaders across the organization. Originally intended to be used as a tool to identify employees with high potential, it has become central to all selection and development systems.

In 1998, Unilever-HPC implemented a competency-based selection system to identify people with the attributes and skills best suited for success at the company. PDP is a company-wide fundamental performance and development process, an important part of which includes competency assessment and development plans. In addition, competency assessment is one of the critical variables used within HRPP, a process that includes identification of high-potential managers, succession planning, and long-term career management for the company's leaders.

Finally, Unilever-HPC offers a number of learning opportunities for employees to improve their competencies. These include a wide variety of didactic and experiential personal development activities.

Endnotes

1. Additional information on this company can be found on the Web at www.unilever.com.

2. *Competencies—Summary* (Unilever Personnel Division, September 1997).

3. *Competency—Dictionary* (Unilever Personnel Division, 1997).

4. *Competencies—Summary* (Unilever Personnel Division, September 1997), 2.

5. *Human Resource Planning Process—Guidelines* (Unilever-HPC—USA, 1999), 7.

6. *Performance Development Planning Facilitator's Guide* (Unilever Home & Personal Care North America, January 1998), 107–108.

W. L. Gore & Associates, Inc.

Company Background

W. L. Gore & Associates, Inc. (Gore), with annual revenues exceeding $1.3 billion, is best known worldwide for its Gore-Tex™ fabrics. Located in more than 45 sites around the world, the company employs more than 6,500 associates. Gore has repeatedly been named as among the "100 Best Companies to Work for in America."[1]

Fundamental to Gore's corporate culture is its passion for product leadership and innovation. The company's team-based environment is designed to encourage product leadership initiatives by fostering direct person-to-person communication. The company emphasizes, "How we work sets us apart.... Our culture is a model for contemporary organizations seeking growth by unleashing creativity and fostering teamwork."[2]

Instead of a hierarchy of bosses and managers, the company's founder, Bill Gore, set out to create a "flat lattice organization." At Gore, there are no chains of command. Nor are there predetermined channels of communication. Leaders at Gore emerge naturally. Leadership is nurtured through learned experiences and an environment that emphasizes fellowship, behaviors, and skills that advance the company's business purposes. How this unique corporate culture translates into the leadership challenges, behavioral expectations, and developmental paths for finance associates at Gore is the emphasis of this case study.

Gore's special culture includes a language of its own. Some of the most important terms used at Gore, which will be found throughout this case study, are defined below.

- *Associate:* All individuals at Gore are equals. There are no titles, job descriptions, or official leaders. The term "employee" is not used at Gore.

- *Commitment:* Each associate makes his or her own commitment to the organization. No associate can impose a commitment on another. All work is organized around teams and commitments. Each commitment is a contract that must be fulfilled before an associate can move on to new or broader responsibilities.

- *Lattice organization:* This term stems from Bill Gore's observation that in every organization there is an underground lattice that disseminates information and gets things done. At Gore, tasks and objectives are not assigned by managers; instead, they are defined by personal commitments and cooperative team efforts.

- *Sponsor:* Every associate has a sponsor. Sponsors are associates who help others to succeed in fulfilling their commitments to both themselves and the organization.

Global Finance and Finance Associates

Since our last visit with Gore in 1994,[3] financial leadership has embraced a more centralized form and emphasis. Finance associate Douglas Maughan notes, "The purpose of establishing the global finance team was not to build a kingdom of financial associates." At Gore, a decentralized or individualistic approach to finance simply did not easily translate into consistent behavioral expectations and developmental paths. More than 225 finance associates currently partner with Gore's businesses and business associates around the world. Maughan adds, "We simply needed a more focused approach to bring everyone along."

The centralization of finance that Maughan describes is far from what one expects. The global financial leadership team is composed of only five finance associates. Two of these associates—one is Maughan—are informally recognized as the leaders of the global financial leadership team. Traditional formal designations, such as CFO, vice president of finance, or controller, do not exist at the company. With the exception of the five members of the global financial leadership team, all finance associates at Gore are integrated into the company's businesses or plant operations. Approximately 10 percent of finance associates at Gore are business analysts focused on developing business metrics, discussed later. The remainder concentrate on transaction processing activities, such as accounts payable, credit, and collections.

In becoming more centralized, the global financial leadership team faced a number of organizational challenges and imperatives:

1. It had to identify and implement core or company-wide practices of measurement, such as the net present value (NPV) of cash flow or the NPV of economic value added. There was also the need to develop metrics more reflective of the critical success factors (CSFs) relevant to each of the company's businesses and product lines around the world. At Gore, where product innovation is fundamental, focusing on the time it takes to bring a product engineer on board is a far more critical metric for enhancing shareholder value than focusing on the cost to hire.

2. With the increased opportunities and demands for finance professionals to partner with the businesses, the global financial leadership team had to develop and implement new behavioral expectations for all finance associates. It needed to develop new tools to communicate these expectations to finance and business associates around the world. At Gore, the most important of these tools is the leadership (or alignment of metrics) pyramid, discussed in the next section.

3. And, with the increased emphasis on reducing financial costs, the company had to "collapse" lower value-added activities. Such initiatives would free Gore's financial executives to provide more leadership value to the businesses. The global financial leadership team needed to implement best practices in the areas of receivables and payables processing, as well as reduce the time it took to close the books each month. With a more centralized approach in place, Gore could aggressively move these changes forward in a more objective, coordinated, and global manner.

A Framework for Financial Leadership

These imperatives capture the essence of the financial leadership challenge at Gore. But the global financial leadership team needed a framework to communicate and turn these challenges into a company-wide reality. That framework had to define and bring together the most important building blocks for the attainment of financial leadership and business success. To this end, the team developed the alignment-of-metrics pyramid, or what we refer to as the Financial Leadership Model (FLM).

With its emphasis on competencies, or "encouraged behaviors," the FLM has become the focal point around which a pragmatic dialogue between finance and business associates at Gore takes place. This dialogue ensures that business people have the right performance metrics in hand to create shareholder value. Moreover, with the growing organizational expectation that such a dialogue will take place, finance people are encouraged to take a proactive leadership role at the company. Maughan emphasizes, "Not only did we want to develop a tool to effectively communicate and establish behavioral expectations for finance associates, but we also wanted to raise the bar of acceptable performance."

The Financial Leadership Model

Figure 11.1 provides a closer look at FLM, specifically, its behavioral and leadership development ramifications for finance associates at Gore.

At the very top of the FLM we find the *purposes of the business.* The most important of these is to enhance shareholder value. Working toward the top of the pyramid, the role of finance is to identify the *performance metrics* that will best promote the *encouraged behaviors* and *critical success factors* for each of the company's businesses. At Gore, the role of finance is to help identify the performance metrics for each of the company's businesses. The goal is to highlight the most appropriate business behaviors to enhance shareholder value.

Each of these building blocks has a specific implication for success in finance. For example, the most important CSF for finance associates is to be at—and to remain at—the business decision-making tables.

Figure 11.1
Alignment of Metrics

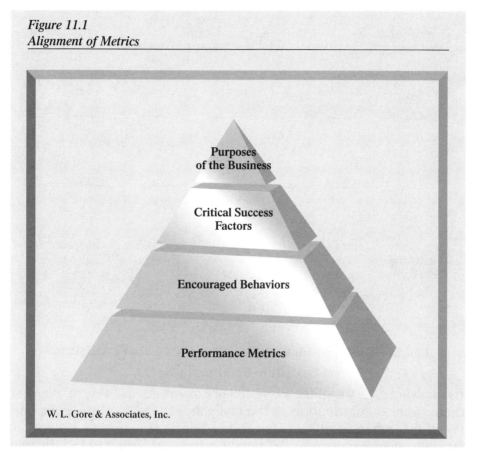

W. L. Gore & Associates, Inc.

Without that opportunity it would be impossible for finance to achieve its purpose, and the foundation of the model would be weak. Accordingly, finance associates are encouraged to display specific behaviors. These behaviors, discussed later, can be found in figure 11.2 Without them, finance would be far less likely to achieve its most important CSF. Once again, this would leave the model with a weak foundation.

Maughan makes this important point: "These interrelationships must not only be articulated and recognized by finance and business associates, but they must also be practiced from the top down and from the bottom up of the model." Thus, demonstrating the appropriate interpersonal behaviors (or competencies) becomes the key to attaining financial leadership at Gore.

Figure 11.2
Developing the Right Metrics for Influencing the Correct Business Behavior

Traditional Metric	Wrong Behavior	Consequence	CSF Metric	Correct Behavior
Cost-to-Hire	Don't advertise	Delays in product launch, loss in final market share	Time-to-Hire	Advertise
Cost Per Salesperson	Reduce support services	Lower sales, loss in market share	Sales contribution	Increase support services
Days Sales Outstanding (DSO)	Increase credit criteria/ restrictions on customers	Create "credit bog" or don't sell	Retention of Customers	Grow sales—more business per loyal customer at lower cost

The CSF for Finance: Securing a Place at the Business Decision-making Table

By applying the logic of the FLM, finance associates are able to increase their business contribution to the company. In the past, the company found that when people did not follow this communicative process, a large divergence occurred: The numbers finance created simply did not influence the right business decisions. Frequently, these decisions led to inappropriate (low value-creating) behaviors, such as focusing too much on collection costs and not enough on the business lost from reduced customer loyalty.

Today, things are very different. Maughan reveals,

> If the metric does not get us the business behavior we want, then we don't measure it, and we don't report it. The problem is getting business people to think about metrics and their business implications. The businesses today that are most successful at Gore are those that clearly see their CSFs. Helping them to do just that,

through the logic of the FLM, is precisely where finance associates can demonstrate real leadership.

By practicing this leadership, finance associates at Gore are able to secure a position at the company's business decision-making table. In Maughan's case, this translates into his participation in Gore's business strategy counsel. For finance associates integrated into the businesses, it means participating as team members in a wide range of business decisions. These decisions include formulating operating budgets, creating marketing plans, and brainstorming on day-to-day business problems. Once at the table, finance can suggest and implement the information and metrics that will allow each business associate or business group to achieve its purpose of creating shareholder value as appropriate for each group. Thus, for finance, securing its place at the decision-making table is the leadership priority.

Maughan concludes,

> No finance associate should be developing metrics in a vacuum. Such metrics just don't work. Business associates need to grasp the implications of the model as it applies to their businesses. Those that see their CSFs—facilitated by finance people—are better performers for the organization. But it is not always easy to get business people to look at their CSFs. Being in a position to both help and influence them to do so is the real leadership challenge we face as finance associates at Gore.

Influencing Businesses to Make the Right Decisions

The following examples show how this leadership process has led to metrics that are influencing business associates at Gore to make the right business decisions. (See figure 11.2.)

For Gore, a crucial business consideration is making sure it hires, as quickly as possible, the best engineers and product developers. If it takes 12 months to hire an engineer, for example, that delay can translate into a 12-month lag in a product launch. Such a postponement can cost the company at least a 3-percent reduction in final market share, or $30,000 on each $1 million in sales. On an annualized basis, this is far more costly than any expenditure for up-front advertising that would be the focus of a cost-to-hire metric. Such a cost-to-hire metric promotes the wrong business behavior for Gore.

Second, the metric of sales contribution (sales minus the variable costs of selling) is far more important than the cost per salesperson. By focusing on selling costs rather than on sales contribution, a reduction in selling expenditures might occur that would lead to a drop in market share—a far more costly consequence to the corporation.

Third, days sales outstanding (DSO) is certainly an important metric. But focusing too much on that metric can lead to inappropriate business behaviors, from a reluctance to sell to decreases in sales caused by too much emphasis on credit criteria. In the process, the far more important metric of customer retention can be lost. Again, by being at the business decision-making table, finance associates can help business leaders identify their CSFs for customer retention and loyalty. This allows finance to influence the more optimal business behavior.

Financial Services Expectations

Clearly, if finance associates at Gore are to make their maximum contribution to the organization, they must be in a leadership position to both help and influence business associates to identify their CSFs. But, says Maughan, "Before the global finance team at Gore was in place, no one had clarified the developmental process of how financial executives move from their traditional role of control and reporting to that of strategic business partner and demonstrated financial leadership."

To rectify this situation, the global financial leadership team, in close collaboration with Gore's HR associates, focused on creating and communicating its Financial Services Expectations (FSE). These expectations focus on three main areas of competence: technical, business knowledge, and interpersonal skills. Most important, they also contain a list of behaviors that an ideal finance associate should demonstrate or develop. With FSE in place, Gore has begun to see a number of developmental benefits.

1. FSE provide a starting point for discussions between finance associates and their sponsors on strengths and weaknesses and alternative paths. There are no formal career paths at Gore.

2. FSE serve as a model to assist finance associates and their sponsors in recognizing what constitutes functional excellence for finance associates and areas for future emphasis.

3. FSE serve as a tool for finance associates to use to assess their own strengths, weaknesses, and future growth.

4. FSE function as guides for writing interview questions for potential finance associate employment candidates, and therefore, establish early on the requisite expectations and behaviors.

FSE are now built into both the hiring and developmental process for all finance associates at Gore. But FSE are not inflexible. In fact, finance associates are not expected to demonstrate or develop all the behaviors. However, with the FSE in place and available for all to view, the expectations of finance associates are clear, and so is the relative importance of each behavior for each area of finance. Moreover, when looking at FSE and demonstrated financial leadership at Gore, certain noteworthy trends and patterns are clearly emerging.

According to Gail Townsend, the HR associate at Gore who works closely with the global financial leadership team,

All three areas—technical, business knowledge, and interpersonal skills—are critical for getting to, and remaining at, the business tables. But increasingly it is the interpersonal behaviors that are surfacing as the key differentiator for the achievement of financial executive leadership. Finance skill competencies are seen as a given. You don't even get interviewed if you don't have them.

At Gore, a leadership transformation has taken place. It is not the finance people with the technical expertise who are successful. Instead, it is the finance people who are in the field, sitting with the business leaders and talking with the customers, and who understand the dynamics of the business and its international aspects. These are the finance associates who are proving themselves to be the company's financial and business leaders. Townsend observes, "It is precisely those finance people who are breaking out of their comfort zone that are increasingly valued by the company and its business associates."

About three years ago, the global financial leadership team came up with the idea of creating its own business plan—one completely separate from, yet supporting, Gore's business plan. This plan is now some 28 pages long and covers all finance activities, from specific best-practice objectives for managing receivables and payables to developmental objectives for finance associates. Every six months the finance team goes over the plan and evaluates what it has or has not accomplished. By implementing its own business plan, the team's finance associates have been able to focus specifically on the contribution they can make to the businesses, as well as stretch their imaginations as to what might be possible. The idea seems to be working.

According to Maughan, "Implementing the plan has been quite refreshing. It has become an important tool for establishing and communicating expectations. With the plan, we have so far saved the organization some $10 million. Some of the savings have been from cost reductions, for example, implementing best practices, and some came about simply because we got better at what we were doing." In short, because finance implemented its own business plan—a rather novel idea—finance associates at Gore can now see what is possible and begin contributing their own vision to the company's expectations.

Breaking Out of the Comfort Zone

It is one thing to recognize and articulate expectations and appropriate behaviors and another to cultivate them. This is a well-recognized reality at Gore. Whether it is to help new finance associates meet the expectations established by FSE or to help existing finance associates break out of their prevailing comfort zones, Gore offers numerous opportunities to its finance professionals.

Leadership Effectiveness Training (LET)[4]
The importance of the softer skills at Gore is demonstrated by the fact that every associate attends a two-and-a-half-day workshop on effective communication. This attendance has been requested directly by the company's founder, Bill Gore. In the halls and meeting rooms at Gore hang framed summaries of the program's key points. Everyone, including visitors, is reminded of the importance of effective communication to the company's leadership development process (figure 11.3).

LET is a workshop forum. It is designed to work on communication skills such as stating needs, listening, negotiating, accepting feedback,

Figure 11.3
Effective Communicating

EFFECTIVE COMMUNICATING
Problem Solving Process

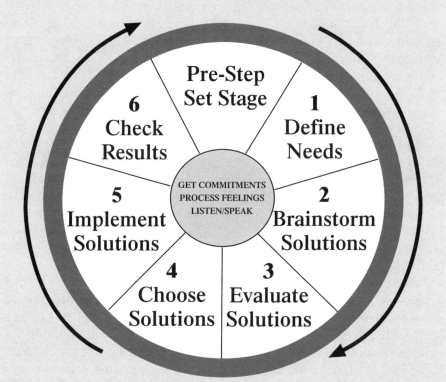

L.E.T. BEHAVIORS

* Send appreciative messages (I-Messages)
* State needs/address issues in a non-confrontational manner (I-Messages)
* Listen to get to core needs/issues and to clarify expectations (Active Listening)
* Negotiate so that everyone's needs are met (Win/Win)
* Accept others' differing points of view (Values Collision)

and sending appreciative messages. LET addresses many of the behaviors that we call leverage competencies. Townsend observes, "If a business or finance associate cannot demonstrate, or simply will not practice, these five behaviors, they reduce the effectiveness of the entire organization."

The LET workshop is based on the assumption that organizations need a new kind of leadership that puts human values first. The emphasis is on developing leadership that facilitates people's creative capacities, the free expression of their individuality, and their active participation in problem solving and goal setting. This is quite different from the traditional notion of leadership, which is based on control. LET presents a model of leadership that is often defined by terms like partnering, collaborative, participative, group-centered, and democratic.

According to Dr. Thomas Gordon, who pioneered the LET program, the move toward participation is the most effective form of leadership in organizations. It is gaining acceptance not only in the United States but throughout the world. He points out that evidence supports its superiority over authoritarian systems of governance. But participative governance requires a new kind of leadership that builds and maintains relationships that are more like partnerships. This philosophy is the entire basis behind Bill Gore's early emphasis on the lattice organization, as well as the importance of communication and a culture free of hierarchy and authoritarian control.

Therefore, when it comes to transforming finance from its traditional roles of control and reporting to that of partnering, influencing, and adding value to the businesses, the values and lessons of LET are right on target. The LET workshop includes six sections emphasizing such communication skills as active listening, influencing others to change behavior, resolving conflicts, handling value collisions, and increasing productive work time. There is also a half-day follow-up session. LET's emphasis on participative governance has proven ideal for finance associates as they struggle with the transition from control and reporting to partnering and teamwork. It represents one of the focal points of leadership development for all associates at Gore.

Townsend explains, "More than skill building, LET is a self-awareness[5] workshop. It is facilitated through an understanding of effective communication. This might include assessing each other in terms of the five behaviors—defining needs, listening, negotiating, accepting feedback, and sending appreciative messages." The program's success is largely derived from the fact that it mixes associates from different commitment areas—20 or so at a time.

Mentors and Sponsors

While LET establishes the mind-set and provides the tools for practicing leadership through effective communication, sponsors and mentors play a significant role in the ongoing leadership development process at Gore. After completing LET, associates are expected to seek out the guidance and work experiences necessary to improve themselves. Here is where mentors and sponsors play a crucial role at Gore. Let's take a look at how sponsors and mentors encourage leadership development in Gore's team-based work environment.

Associates must have a sponsor from the very beginning of their careers at Gore. Initially, these sponsors are assigned; however, as their commitment to the organization grows or changes, associates are free to change their sponsors. In this regard, the role of the sponsor in the development process of each associate is taken very seriously. Sponsors are responsible for both the performance and leadership growth of each of their associates.

It is important to recognize that sponsorship selection is not tied to functional expertise. While a finance associate may seek out many mentors, including those with financial skills and backgrounds, it would not be unusual for the same finance associate to select a sponsor who is a recognized nonfinance business leader in the organization. The sponsor's role is not to focus on an associate's technical skills. Instead, it is to ensure that an associate is exposed to the team-based work experiences he or she needs to grow and make a larger contribution to the organization. In summary, associates look to their sponsors not so much for technical expertise as for feedback,[6] behavioral guidance, and exposure to team-based work experiences that will broaden their contribution to the organization.

Maughan notes,

> For finance associates, we ask their sponsors to go through the FSE and see where they are, or are not, using 360-degree feedback and other assessment tools. If an associate is in trouble, it is up to the sponsor to determine how to get him or her out of the weeds by

identifying the proper work experiences. This process of focusing on the expectations, the feedback, and the requisite experiences emphasizes an associate's developmental path and a more realistic assessment of the associate's abilities. There is no such thing as a career path at Gore. It is up to the sponsors to help associates move on to a broader commitment in the organization.

One final point: Becoming a sponsor is considered to be part of demonstrated leadership at Gore. It is an opportunity, not a right. Associates cannot ask to be sponsors, nor can associates be promoted to sponsor roles. It is not a promotion tool. A sponsor must be asked to play that role by another associate. How a sponsor fulfills this responsibility plays a large part in that person's performance and compensation review. For example, when ranking an associate's contribution against that of all others in the organization—a practice at Gore—effectiveness as a sponsor is an important component.

Developing Financial Leadership: Final Thoughts and Practices

Clearly, the road to financial leadership at Gore is fully captured by the FLM. With the FSE, LET, sponsors, mentors, and the constant reinforcement of team-based work experiences, Gore is transforming the role of finance associates into one of business leadership and creativity. But there is still more to be said about how financial leadership is emerging and developing at Gore.

To begin with, there is the role and importance of vision to financial leadership. The leaders of the global financial leadership team readily admit that vision is not always a comfortable subject for finance associates to discuss. Maughan observes,

> Vision is real tough for most finance people. But the successful finance people today are the ones that can look beyond just putting out fires. Today, we are asking finance associates to map out and improve processes. If you don't have the vision, you can't do this. Vision is one of the things we are trying to develop in our finance associates. We believe it can be developed and fostered—at least to some extent, anyway.

When it comes to developing vision and effectiveness in finance associates, two additional points need to be stressed.

First, while Gore's finance leaders clearly think that vision can be nurtured, they also believe strongly that finance associates must be exposed to numerous business experiences to help bring their vision to the surface. Townsend explains, "Getting successful experiences under one's belt is far more critical to the developmental process than any single course or seminar. This is a team sport and if an associate opts out of the team, he or she won't make it."

Second, the finance leaders at Gore strongly believe that there is an inherent conflict between vision and organizational size. Maughan observes, "You can't develop and implement financial best practices for an organization like Gore while at the same time trying to build a financial kingdom."

The Role of Competencies: Making the Transition

Since our visit with Gore in 1994, the company has made tremendous strides in financial leadership development. Finance plays a significant influencing role in making both day-to-day and longer-term strategic business decisions. By fostering effective communication between finance and business associates, finance has gained a recognized place at the company's business decision-making table. Today there is a clear road map in place for practicing and developing financial leadership. This is embodied in FLM and FSE as well as in the numerous mechanisms to facilitate financial leadership development, such as LET and the sponsorship program.

However, financial associate development at Gore is still a work in progress. With FSE in place, HR and finance are now actively seeking to create a refined list of competencies essential for effectively practicing financial leadership. According to Townsend, "It is becoming evident that articulating a smaller set of essential competencies is very advantageous. In some respects, they are a common ground across all business areas and functions. The behaviors in our FSE are a good starting point for finance. Emphasizing the competencies will make it easier for finance associates to understand what it takes to be successful. It should boil down to about five to seven."

In terms of moving from behaviors to competencies, Townsend provides a powerful set of reasons for making this list of competencies the next logical step:

1. They can be used as a baseline to hire finance associates.

2. They are the criteria for building a sense of self-awareness.

3. They are critical for helping sponsors evaluate the performance of finance associates.

4. They are essential for developmental planning.

Summary

■ Effective communication and a sense of self-awareness are essential to the leadership development of finance associates at Gore. Increasingly, financial skills are seen as a given, while interpersonal behaviors are becoming the differentiating factor for achieving leadership.

■ To encourage these softer competencies and leadership behaviors, all associates at Gore, including finance associates, take part in LET—at the direct request of the founder of the company.

■ Recognizing the importance of effective communication to the leadership process, Gore's global financial leadership team has developed a special model—the FLM. The model links the importance of an organization's purposes to critical success factors and requisite behaviors. It can be applied to an entire organization, its individual businesses, or to finance itself. The model has brought about a greater appreciation and broader leadership role for finance.

■ To ensure that finance maintains its place at the company's business decision-making table—finance's most important CSF—Gore has developed its financial services expectations. FSE articulate the requisite behaviors, and their relative importance, for attaining technical business knowledge, and interpersonal competencies. FSE have been incorporated into the hiring, ongoing evaluation, and developmental paths of all financial associates.

- Every finance associate at Gore has a sponsor. Sponsors are critical to the leadership process. They help associates identify their strengths and weaknesses, using FSE and 360-degree feedback, and they provide developmental guidance.

- A finance associate's sponsor need not come from finance. In fact, this is typically not the case. A finance associate has only one sponsor, but he or she may have many mentors. Mentors can be sought out for their functional expertise, knowledge of a specific business, or a particular behavioral competency.

- Although LET and FSE are important for building the foundation of financial leadership, seeking out team-based work experiences is considered the most important element of leadership development. Finance associates cannot broaden their commitment to the organization without getting out of their comfort zones.

- Gore has taken giant steps forward in its approach to finance associate leadership development. Nevertheless, the company still sees its efforts as a work in progress. While FSE clearly articulate important behaviors, including the softer stuff of financial leadership, the next step is to boil them down into a smaller set of competencies that embrace all the essential components of FSE.

Endnotes

1. *Fortune* magazine commissioned Robert Levering and Milton Moskowitz to compile the list beginning in 1998. Gore appeared as one of the top 20 in the 1999 list. Gore was also included in their two previous books, *The 100 Best Companies to Work for in America,* making it one of a select group of fewer than 20 companies to be noted in all four places.

2. For more background information, visit the company's Web site at www.wlgore.com.

3. In 1994, the Research Foundation published *The Empowered Organization: Redefining the Roles and Practices of Finance.* Gore was featured as one of a select group of companies that had early on embraced a new vision for finance—as a true and equal partner with its businesses.

4. LET, developed by Gordon Training International, was brought in house by Gore ten years ago. Today the workshop is entirely facilitated by Gore's HR associates. Figure 11.3, and some of the references herein, were adapted from the workshop materials of Dr. Thomas Gordon.

5. Our research indicates that "self-awareness" is one of the most important of the leverage competencies. For more of an explanation of self-awareness, see the exhibit on leverage competencies in appendix A.

6. Gore uses a wide variety of techniques to ensure that all associates have the most extensive feedback regarding their performance and contribution to the organization, including such mechanisms as 360-degree feedback.

Research Questionnaire Protocol

Research Description and Purpose

The business mandate to reinforce and expand finance into a force of organizational change and business effectiveness has clearly been placed on the table; however, without the requisite competencies—or blueprint to achieve them—there is a significant chance that financial executives may not be able to meet the business and leadership tasks at hand.

Accordingly, this FERF research study seeks to examine the formidable challenges currently faced by financial executives, and to clearly identify critical competencies that financial executives are required to possess to successfully meet them.

Moreover, the research will uncover how these competencies are being addressed and developed by a wide range of organizations—by financial executives individually, and in conjunction with others within their organizations, i.e., most specifically, with business line managers and human resource executives.

Instructions to Protocol User

In our interviews with your organization we will be speaking with executives from your finance, human resource, and business line operations. The total time required to complete all interviews at your organization should be approximately one-half to a full day, with individual interviews lasting a maximum of two hours.

Although the interviews will take the form of a discussion or dialogue, the questions on the next page will give you a good indication of the areas that we will specifically be covering during our interviews. It would be greatly appreciated if you could take some time to review this protocol prior to your scheduled interview with the FERF researchers. However, this pre-interview should take no more than an hour of your time. Also, by no means feel obligated to actually answer these questions prior to the on-site interview.

Most of the questions in this protocol will apply to all executives at your organization participating in this research. However, there are a number of questions that may only apply to financial executives *(FE)*, human resource personnel *(HR)*, and/or business line management *(LM)*. These questions are indicated in *italics*.

Protocol Questions

I. Overview

1. What are the greatest challenges confronting financial executives at your organization?

2. How do these challenges differ for the CFO, treasurer, controller, etc.?

3. Are these challenges effectively being met? Are some being met better than others? Why or why not?

4. Have you seen any trends or patterns in the qualities of finance people who "succeed" or "fail"? Can you cite some specific examples?

5. What are the positive things about your finance organization that enable it to make a contribution to the business?

II. Identifying Critical Skills and Competencies and Their Impact

1. **Please see the attached table and descriptions of "leverage competencies" (EXHIBIT A).** In your opinion, which of these competencies are most important for the success of financial executives? Are there any which should be added to the list? Deleted?

2. Please give examples of how possessing leverage competencies have helped financial executives in your organization effectively impact the business?

3. Please give examples of how lacking some of these competencies has hindered financial executives in your organization.

4. *Think of the most effective finance person you have ever worked with. What, in your opinion, made them so effective? (LM)*

5. *What would make it easier to partner with finance people within your organization? (LM)*

6. What kinds of business events, interactions, or feedback indicate to you that finance people need improvement in these competencies?

7. Is there any specific type of work (e.g., budgeting, strategic planning, cost management, audit and control) in which certain leverage competencies may be especially important? Please give examples.

8. *Do you believe that certain leverage competencies have contributed to your ability to impact the business? Which ones? Why? (FE)*

9. *Have some become more critical in recent years? Which do you expect to become more important in the new millennium? (FE)*

10. *What competencies do you wish you could have been "better" at earlier in you career? What competencies do you still wish you could improve? (FE)*

11. Overall, what leverage competencies or personal qualities would you look for if you were hiring financial executives?

12. *In the recruiting/hiring process, are these competencies taken into account? If so, how? (FE, HR)*

13. *In terms of the evaluative/promotion process, are these competencies taken into account? If so, how? (FE, HR)*

14. *Can you recount a specific situation which went especially well for you, or you felt particularly effective...a high point? (FE)*

15. *Can you discuss an experience in which you felt you were not as effective as you could be...a low point? (FE)*

III. Developing Requisite Skills and Competencies

1. Which leverage competencies may be developed through time and experience?

2. Which leverage competencies may be acquired through training and development?

3. Does your company emphasize the importance of leverage competencies in the development and effectiveness of its finance people? In what specific ways? What does your organization do to help its financial executives (or others) gain leverage competencies?

4. With regard to leverage competencies, does your organization provide:

   - external training courses (sending people to public courses/ workshops)?

   - internal training courses (courses provided by your organization's training group)?

   - internal mentoring programs?

   - executive coaching programs?

   - other programs or development opportunities?

5. If so, how have they been helpful or not helpful? Have they just been "feel-good" programs without any long-lasting effects? Or, have they provided skills/competencies that have a direct or indirect impact on one's career development, performance, or quality of work life?

6. If so, how often are these courses or programs given? Are they required and to what extent must you attend or participate in them on an annual basis?

7. Which courses or development opportunities have you seen to be most effective? Please give examples of programs and the competencies that they enhanced.

8. Are there any types of leverage competency training which should be mandatory for certain financial executives?

9. Are there any assessment processes or procedures utilized to assess a financial executive's leverage competencies (e.g., 360-degree feedback, a "competency audit")? If not, should there be and if so, how?

10. Are there any experiences, changes, or initiatives that an organization might do to promote the development of leverage competencies outside of specific training opportunities (e.g., increased participation in cross functional groups or small business units)?

11. What is the appropriate career balance and progression between traditional financial skills and leverage competencies? In embracing both financial skills and leverage competencies, what should a personal development plan look like for a financial executive over the course of his/her career?

IV. Major Obstacles and Barriers

1. Do you believe that leverage competencies are more readily discussed and practiced in certain areas of the organization than in other areas? Do financial executives stress these competencies more, less, or the same as others?

2. Within your organization, what are the greatest barriers to the development and/or utilization of a financial executive's leverage competencies?

3. Within your organization, what are the greatest barriers to finance's ability to achieve business effectiveness?

4. *To what extent does the increased demand for financial executives to empower, partner, integrate, etc., lead to increased job-related stress?* **(FE, HR)**

5. *How is this stress manifesting itself in the performance etc., of financial executives? How are these job related impacts of stress being addressed in your organization?* **(FE, HR)**

V. Future Trends and Directions

1. Does anything else come to mind about the competencies required by financial executives or how they are acquired?

2. Are there any questions or concerns you would add to this protocol regarding the future roles and behaviors of finance at your organization?

3. If you had to identify one major business trend or development that is likely to impact the effectiveness of financial executives at your organization in the new millennium, what would it be? Are you optimistic or pessimistic with regard to your finance organization's ability to meet this challenge? Why or why not?

4. Do you believe that the rapid technological developments taking place in communications, computers, and the Internet will increase the relative importance of leverage competencies? Why or why not, and in what specific ways?

5. What other events or circumstances do you see impacting the future and relative importance of leverage competencies? In what specific ways are these developments likely to impact financial executives? How would you suggest such executives prepare for these developments?

Exhibit A

Leverage Competencies

Below is a list of "leverage" competencies. These are "soft" skills, qualities, and abilities that are believed to be increasingly important for an individual's success in an organization. Current surveys indicate that traditional "hard" skills and competencies (e.g., technical knowledge) are necessary but not sufficient for the leadership success of a financial executive and his/her organization. Individuals and companies who leverage the advantage of these competencies are expected to be the most successful in the future.

The list below is not intended to be all-inclusive, and many competencies overlap with one another. These noted competencies are intended to facilitate discussion during our interview. You may, of course, wish to include competencies not listed here.

Adaptability—Flexibility in managing change and challenges. Ability to adapt to and work effectively in a variety of situations. Ability to quickly integrate new ideas, approaches, and information.

Assertiveness—Ability to effectively "stand up" for one's beliefs and ideas, while also appreciating the concerns of others.

Conflict Management—Negotiating and resolving disagreements. Ability to handle difficult situations and facilitate "win-win" solutions.

Communication—Effectively using verbal and written communication. Formal or informal. Articulating relevant ideas and information. Fostering open communication. Skill at giving and receiving feedback. Being a "good listener."

Consulting Skills—Ability to effectively identify customer's underlying issues and generate practical and creative solutions that are successfully implemented.

Cooperation—Ability to effectively work with others toward shared goals.

Customer Orientation—Anticipating, recognizing, and meeting customers' (internal or external) needs.

Expectations Management—Setting the appropriate level of expectations regarding goals and outcomes among customers, clients, and coworkers.

Influence—Ability to influence others to appreciate one's point of view and cooperate with efforts of the team or organization.

Interpersonal Understanding—Ability to understand the attitudes, interests, needs, and perspectives of others. Understand complex, underlying reasons for the actions of others.

Leadership—Ability to inspire and manage individuals and groups regardless of reporting relationships. Articulate a vision and arouse enthusiasm.

Managing/Leveraging Diversity—The ability to interact effectively with people from different backgrounds, cultures, or countries and use those differences for business advantage.

Relationship Building—Building appropriate networks and alliances to effectively get one's work done.

Self-confidence/Optimism—Demonstrating confidence in ability to reach goals despite obstacles, setbacks, or failures.

Self-control—Ability to keep calm and steady in the face of opposition, frustration, or stress.

Stress Management—Coping with job-related and personal stress. "Mental toughness."

Glossary

Assessment center. Assessment centers evaluate groups of individuals on multiple dimensions, using several assessment methods and raters. Assessment may include a variety of paper and pencil questionnaires, group and individual interviews, and various job-simulation exercises that may be done individually or in groups.

Behavioral event job interview. This form of job interview involves evaluating job candidates on a number of dimensions, usually competency-based, by focusing on specific behaviors. Questions seek behavioral examples of a candidate's past job performance. These questions ask what candidates would do in hypothetical situations or what they have done in the past. Questions and rating criteria are developed in advance.

Coaching. Coaching is a learning process designed to bring about improved performance and effectiveness at work and personal growth leading to better leadership skills. Coaching is done on an individual basis. A company may employ professional *executive coaches* to work with its leaders. Coaching also may be available in-house through human resources (HR) or related departments. Some organizations train managers or **mentors** in coaching skills.

Cognitive competencies. Competencies or skills that specifically refer to intellectual capabilities. Such competencies are assumed to be an expression of one's underlying intelligence or intelligence quotient (IQ). IQ represents one's potential for acquiring cognitive competencies. These may be as simple as reading or performing arithmetic, or they may be more complex competencies, such as analytic thinking.

Competencies. Personal characteristics or sets of habits that are related to effective job performance. These traits or sets of habits involve stable, enduring patterns or styles of behavior, thought, and emotions.

Competency model. A model that identifies the competencies important for successful or superior performance in a given job, profession, or organization. The competencies are defined as concretely as possible, and examples of behaviors that demonstrate each competency are provided.

Corporate culture. A stable pattern of an organization's values, beliefs, goals, practices, and customs. The organization's culture directly influences the leverage competencies that the organization values. Leverage competencies of organizational leaders, in turn, influence the corporate culture.

Critical success factors. The factors determined to be critical for the success of a business. They may be companywide or identified for specific departments or functions. For example, a critical success factor frequently identified for finance has been "having a place at the business decision-making table." Specific behaviors may be identified as facilitating these factors, which, in turn, facilitate organizational goals.

Emotional intelligence. The capacity for managing one's emotions, behaviors, and relationships with others. Also known as emotional quotient (EQ). This is taken from IQ, which represents a global measurement of classic intelligence. Emotional intelligence is expressed through a variety of **emotional competencies.** Research indicates that EQ is a better predictor than IQ of success on the job.

Emotional competencies. Characteristics and capabilities based on underlying emotional intelligence. These learned capabilities include thoughts, feelings, and behaviors. Emotional competencies represent the great majority of competencies that have been identified as distinguishing superior from average work performance.

Emotionally intelligent organization. An organization that displays **emotional competencies** on a systemwide basis. For example, an emotionally intelligent individual will display good communication skills. An emotionally intelligent corporation will foster effective communication throughout the organization.

Foundation competencies. Competencies that are necessary but not sufficient for superior job performance. The traditional finance skills and competencies are the foundation for successful job performance, but many believe that they are no longer sufficient for true finance leadership in an organization. See also **threshold competencies.**

High potentials. Some companies attach this label to employees, usually at the management level, who are expected to advance to more senior levels of leadership. In companies that use competency models, employees may be rated against job skills and competencies to see if they are performing at the level of their current job or at a higher level job. If they are demonstrating the competencies of the higher level, they are deemed high potential and are expected to advance to the more senior level within the foreseeable future.

Leverage competencies. Competencies that differentiate superior from average job performance. Although **foundation** or **threshold competencies** are necessary for financial executives to attain minimal levels of job performance, leverage competencies are those required to reach true finance leadership in an organization.

Mentor. A person in an organization who takes responsibility for providing individual attention to facilitate the professional development of another member of the organization. The mentor is at a more senior level of the company but is not necessarily the supervisor of the person being mentored or even from the same department. An employee may have more than one mentor, and the relationship may be formal or informal. Also see **sponsor.**

Operationalize. The process of defining a concept in terms of behaviors that are objective and measurable. This process is instrumental in making the soft skills hard. Competencies must be operationalized to identify relevant ones, evaluate them, and monitor their development.

Performance review and development planning. Companies typically have a process that involves assessing employees against a variety of criteria and performance goals. Plans are developed that outline the employee's specific professional goals and the means to reach them. Professional goals are often tied to organizational goals. This process is usually performed annually, with a number of follow-ups throughout the year. Companies with competency-based performance and development planning assess employees against relevant professional skills and competencies and center development plans around these competencies.

Position profiles (also known as *role profiles*). Some companies develop specific profiles for a variety of positions. These profiles may include responsibilities, skills, competencies, and specific behaviors expected to be demonstrated for a given role.

Selection. A company's hiring process or processes. Competency-based selection systems involve identifying candidates who are strongest in a number of leverage competencies that have been identified as critical for a given position. Competency-based interviews (see **behavioral event job interviews**) and **assessment centers** may be used to evaluate candidates against the relevant competencies.

Sponsor. A formalized mentoring role (see **mentor**). A sponsor is responsible for the professional development of the sponsored associate. He or she need not be a supervisor or even from the same department. (See the W. L. Gore & Associates, Inc. case study for a discussion of sponsors.)

Succession planning. The process of determining an organization's future leaders. This may involve identifying **high potentials.** Companies use a variety of methods for succession planning. Some companies are now incorporating assessment of key leverage competencies in their decision-making process.

360-degree feedback. An evaluation and feedback process that involves gathering detailed information from an individual's supervisor(s), subordinates, and associates. It may be conducted by an in-house professional (in human resources) or by an outside consultant. It may be global in nature or focused on specific issues or competencies.

Threshold competencies. Basic competencies that are necessary for an individual to perform a given job. Such competencies, such as being able to read or do arithmetic, must be present for minimal job performance but will not distinguish average from star performers. Also see **foundation competencies.**

Annotated Bibliography

Stephen Barr. "Sometimes a Great Notion" *CFO* (May 1998): 41–50.

This is a valuable overview of some of the recent training and development endeavors being undertaken by companies on behalf of their financial executives. It covers a wide spectrum of companies and situations, from Procter & Gamble's Finance College to TRW's alliance with the Fuqua School of Business in developing a five-day training seminar called creating strategic partnerships. The article does not go into great detail on competencies or their development, but it clearly highlights the major investment that organizations are making to develop their financial executives as potential leaders—and initiators of change—at their organizations.

Henry A. Davis and Frederick C. Militello, Jr. *The Empowered Organization: Redefining the Roles and Practices of Finance* (Morristown, NJ: Financial Executives Research Foundation, 1994).

This is one of the first books published to explore the changing role of the financial executive in organizational life. With an emphasis on defining a new paradigm for financial work—including teamwork, information sharing, empowerment, and managing by values—the research examined the practices of nine major organizations committed to getting their financial executives out of their "silos" and integrated into their company's businesses. Although the study focused on new behaviors and set the stage for new expectations, it did not examine the development process or skills that financial executives required to meet those challenges. W. L. Gore participated in this study. Because of Gore's earlier participation and the accolades it recently has received for consistently being one of the best companies to work for in America, the researchers selected Gore as a participant in this current research.

S. Ghoshal and C. Bartlett. *The Individualized Corporation: A Fundamentally New Approach to Management* (New York: HarperCollins, 1997).

Based on six years of research and interviews with hundreds of executives from organizations such as Asea Brown Boveri, Intel, General Electric, and Unilever, this book provides tremendous insight into the importance of the individual as the driver of value creation. According to the authors, corporate leaders must recognize that human creativity and individual initiative are their most important sources of competitive advantage in today's global market arena. This book was important in helping the researchers select companies for this study, such as Unilever, because it laid the groundwork for the next logical question: How do these leading organizations encourage and develop the requisite competencies to make the individualized corporation a working reality?

Daniel Goleman. *Working with Emotional Intelligence* (New York: Bantam Books, 1998).

Daniel Goleman is considered the leading authority on emotional intelligence and emotional competencies. Emotional intelligence— how well we manage ourselves and our relationships—is a better predictor of job success than intelligence. Emotional competencies are characteristics and capabilities that are based on one's underlying emotional intelligence. It is mastery of these competencies that distinguishes star performers in any field, and the higher up one goes in an organization, the more important emotional intelligence becomes. Emotional intelligence may be improved at any stage in one's career, and Goleman offers guidelines for training in emotional competencies. He also discusses the value of an emotionally intelligent organization.

Daniel Goleman. "What Makes a Leader?" *Constructor* (May 1999): 14–26.

This article is an excellent introduction for those seeking a shorter version of Goleman's book and a summary of the competencies he identifies as most important for leadership success. Its main theme is simple: IQ and technical skills are important, but emotional intelligence is the *sine qua non* of leadership.

Thomas Gordon. *Leadership Effectiveness Training: The Foundation for Participative Management and Employee Evolvement* (New York: G. P. Putnam's Sons, 1977).

Now in its twenty-first printing, this book is clearly a classic on the interpersonal leadership skills necessary for making participative management—employee participation and involvement in problem solving and decision-making—a reality for organizations. Today, nearly 10,000 managers and supervisors attend the LET workshop, based on the book, annually. This book is included here because it is core to the leadership development approach at W. L. Gore. In fact, all associates at Gore are required by the CEO to attend a LET workshop as part of their leadership development.

Micheline Maynard. *The Global Manufacturing Vanguard: New Rules from the Industry Elite* (New York: John Wiley & Sons, 1998).

This book focuses on a group of companies that the author refers to as the "global manufacturing vanguard." These companies are setting new industry standards by combining clearly conceived processes, leading-edge technology, and seamless people management emphasizing values, courageous leadership, and innovative directions. Its focus is on global managers and the skills and competencies it takes to make a competitive difference. Highly related to our study, the book places a great deal of emphasis on the leadership practices at Dana Corporation.

Mark Nevins and Stephen A. Stumpf. "21st Century Leadership: Redefining Management Education." *Business Strategy,* no. 16 (third quarter 1999): 41–51.

This article, published in Booz-Allen & Hamilton's monthly strategy journal, sets the stage for the leadership competencies required for the twenty-first century. Besides Goleman's work, it is one of the few references that actually articulates these competencies, from strategic focus and vision to flexibility and adaptability. It also suggests a new management education framework to make them a reality for organizations. For example, it emphasizes the importance of getting leaders to teach other leaders, one of the main themes brought out in this research and especially highlighted by the case of Bristol-Myers Squibb. The article is an excellent addendum to our research and its findings.

Price Waterhouse Financial and Cost Management Team. *CFO: Architect of the Corporation's Future* (New York: John Wiley & Sons, 1997).

Based on research with over 300 CFOs from around the world and subsequently published by the Conference Board, this book presents a vision for what is possible when finance changes its focus from a force of control and reporting to one of leading change initiatives and becoming real partners with the organization's CEOs (and businesses). The book was inspirational to us in highlighting the importance of leverage competencies as one of the areas that needed the most attention by CFOs to make this new vision a reality. Moreover, it suggested that the development of such competencies was perhaps one of the areas most neglected by CFOs.

Lyle M. Spencer and Signe M. Spencer. *Competence at Work: Models for Superior Job Performance* (New York: John Wiley & Sons, 1993).

The authors describe in detail a rigorous methodology for job competence assessment. They provide a competency dictionary for 21 competencies that have been found to differentiate superior from average job performance in a variety of fields. The book outlines generic competency models for technicians and professionals, salespeople, helping and human service workers, managers, and entrepreneurs. Applications of their work to recruitment, assessment, selection, succession planning, career path development, performance management, training and development, and competency-based pay are all described. This book is especially valuable for HR professionals.

Frederick Charles Militello, Jr., has co-authored two FEI publications: *The Empowered Organization: Redefining the Roles and Practices of Finance* and *Foreign Exchange Risk Management: A Survey of Corporate Practices.* The Foundation has also just published his most recent work, *Reassessing Corporate Banking Relationships: Practices, Issues, and New Directions.* Mr. Militello has more than 20 years' experience as a financial advisor, entrepreneur, and financial executive. He has been a vice president and managing director for the Chase Manhattan Bank as well as holding financial executive positions for Business International Corporation, Mobil Oil, and USS Corporation. He is currently president of FinQuest Partners LLC and adjunct professor of international business at New York University's Leonard N. Stern Graduate School of Business. Mr. Militello also sits on the boards of many e-technology companies.

Michael D. Schwalberg, Ph.D., has worked with a wide range of clients in developing the skills and tools necessary to implement leverage business competencies—including executives from some of the world's leading organizations, such as American Express, Banco Popular, Bristol Myers, and Unilever. He graduated Phi Beta Kappa from Emory University, received his doctorate in psychology from the State University of New York at Albany, and interned at Brown University. Dr. Schwalberg has worked on research projects at Brown University, the State University of New York at Albany, Fairleigh Dickinson University, and the New York Hospital—Cornell Medical Center. Currently, he is a partner at Hudson Valley Psychology Associates, PLLC, where he provides consultation, counseling, and coaching services.

ACKNOWLEDGMENTS

The authors would like to thank all the financial executives who participated in this study and who provided their valuable time, thoughts, and energies to bring it to a successful completion. These executives include the following:

At Air Products and Chemicals, Inc., Mark Bye, vice president and general manager, Performance Chemicals Division; Paul Huck, vice president and corporate controller; and Jay McAndrew, vice president, human resources.

At Bristol-Myers Squibb, Michael F. Mee, senior vice president and chief financial officer; Frederick S. Schiff, vice president controller; and Sandra Holleran, vice president human resources.

At Dana Corporation, John (Jack) Simpson, executive vice president and chief financial officer (retired); Duncan James, of Dana University; and Melvin H. Rothlisberger, vice president, corporate audit.

At Nortel Networks Corporation, Carl Marcotte, director of credit management; Katherine Parker, director, business effectiveness; and Kate Stevenson, treasurer.

At Synovus Financial Corp., Stephanie Alford, EVP; Walter Deriso, Jr., vice chairman of the Board; Elizabeth R. James, vice chairman; and William Nigh, senior vice president.

At Solvay Polymers, Inc., Guy H. Mercier, vice president finance.

At Unilever Home & Personal Care—USA, James Conti, human resource director for finance; Paul Garwood, president and chief operating officer, Laundry Business Unit; Mark Landry, senior vice president finance; and Greg Polcer, vice president finance.

At W. L. Gore and Associates, Inc., Douglas R. Maughan, finance associate; and Gail Townsend, human resource associate.

We would also like to extend our special gratitude to the project's advisory committee (listed on page iii) as well as to all the members of the Financial Executives Research Foundation, especially our project manager, Cynthia Waller Vallario, and Gracie F. Hemphill, director—research, who guided the work on to its publication. Also we wish to extend our gratitude to Rhona L. Ferling, publications manager, who made many substantive suggestions during the draft manuscript stages

ACKNOWLEDGMENTS

of production. Finally, we wish to thank the president of Financial Executives International, Philip B. Livingston, for his continued support for the publication of this research and his commitment and encouragement to the leadership development of all financial executives.